THE REVISED VERSION
EDITED FOR THE USE OF SCHOOLS

ISAIAH
I—XXXIX

ISAIAH
I—XXXIX

EDITED BY

THE REV. C. H. THOMSON, M.A.

AND

THE REV. JOHN SKINNER, D.D.

CAMBRIDGE
AT THE UNIVERSITY PRESS
1910

CAMBRIDGE
UNIVERSITY PRESS

University Printing House, Cambridge CB2 8BS, United Kingdom

Published in the United States of America by Cambridge University Press, New York

Cambridge University Press is part of the University of Cambridge.

It furthers the University's mission by disseminating knowledge in the pursuit of education, learning and research at the highest international levels of excellence.

www.cambridge.org
Information on this title: www.cambridge.org/9781107649439

© Cambridge University Press 1910

First published 1910
First paperback edition 2014

A catalogue record for this publication is available from the British Library

ISBN 978-1-107-64943-9 Paperback

PREFACE BY THE GENERAL EDITOR
FOR THE OLD TESTAMENT

THE aim of this series of commentaries is to explain the Revised Version for young students, and at the same time to present, in a simple form, the main results of the best scholarship of the day.

The General Editor has confined himself to supervision and suggestion. The writer is, in each case, responsible for the opinions expressed and for the treatment of particular passages.

A. H. M^CNEILE.

January, 1910.

CONTENTS

INTRODUCTION

I. Isaiah's personal history and characteristics.

Isaiah (whose name signifies "salvation of Yahwe[1]")
was the son of Amoz (of whom nothing further is known),
and was born, in all probability, about the year 770 B.C.
His prophetic activity began (vi. 1) in the year of Uzziah's
death (c. 740 B.C.), and continued until 701 B.C., the year
of Sennacherib's unsuccessful attempt to reduce Jerusalem.
None of his discourses can with any degree of plausibility
be assigned to the period subsequent to Sennacherib's
retreat, and the late tradition that he suffered martyrdom
by being sawn asunder in the reign of Manasseh has
no secure foundation. Isaiah's public career, therefore,
coincided with the last forty years of the eighth century
B.C., and in the political history of his country during
these eventful years he played an important part. He
held no office, either secular or ecclesiastical ; his position
was that of an independent adviser, who spoke, as he
conceived, in the name, and with the authority, of God.
His intense conviction that the Divine authority was
absolute over national as well as personal actions and
relations, and that Israel stood or fell politically according
to the measure of the people's faith and obedience, along
with his keen political insight and deep interest in the
national welfare, constrained him to enter the political

[1] This form, now generally accepted as correct, is used
throughout this book instead of Jehovah (regularly rendered in
the text "the Lord").

arena, and made him a statesman as well as a preacher. The record of his public life (see § III) is thus very largely the history of the political movements of his time.

Of Isaiah's family and personal history little is known. He was married (viii. 3), and had at least two sons, to whom he gave symbolic names (vii. 3 : viii. 3). That he was of good social position may be inferred from his easy intercourse with the king (vii. 3), and other persons of repute (viii. 2), from his intimate acquaintance with the social life of the capital, with the inner side of politics and the intrigues of the court, from his contempt for low-born upstarts like Pekah (vii. 4) and Shebna (xxii. 16), as well as from the general impression to be gathered from his writings or addresses that he was a man of broad culture and belonged to the educated and governing class. He was a citizen of Jerusalem, and loved his city with a passionate devotion. It was his own city, the historic capital of his nation, the city of Yahwe and of the Messianic king. His sympathies, however, were broad, and he was no mere townsman. On the contrary, he took a keen interest in rural life and in the various operations of agriculture, which supplied him with many telling similes and illustrations (e.g. i. 8 : v. 1–7 : xvii. 5 f. : xxviii. 23–29). A whole-hearted and unselfish lover of his country, Isaiah nevertheless incurred the odium of want of patriotism. The intensity of his religious convictions and his sincerity of thought and feeling forbade him to adopt the motto "my country right or wrong," and throughout the whole, or almost the whole, of his career, his country was, according to his profound conviction, on the all-important question of the national attitude to God, fundamentally in the wrong (see §§ II, IV). He was therefore in sharp and consistent opposition to all the opportunists, shallow optimists, and "hurra-patriots" of his time. From his own secure standing-ground of faith he opposed alike their foolish boasting (xxviii. 5–16:

xxx. 15-17), and their lapses into craven fear (vii. 1-9).
On social and economic questions also Isaiah was brought
into conflict with the great majority of the ruling class.
He was attached to the old order (see § II), with its free
proprietors cultivating the soil, and its comparatively even
distribution of wealth, and he sympathised strongly with
the poor, and with the victims of injustice and oppression.
With the bulk of the official religious leaders of the
people, the priests and the prophets, Isaiah had little in
common. He hated their superficial formalism, their
sensuality, and the venal complaisance with which they
prophesied smooth things (xxix. 13 : xxviii. 7 : xxx. 10).
The mass of the people followed only too readily the guidance of their political, social, and religious leaders, and for
the most part turned a deaf ear to the prophet's warnings
and exhortations. Encountering on every side either active
hostility or the resistance of inertia, Isaiah could not but
be a severe critic of his countrymen, and his addresses
consist in preponderating measure of warning and invective. He could not conceal from himself the fact that
he was a voice crying in the wilderness, and he cherished
no delusive hopes of success (vi. 9 ff.). In these circumstances it is noteworthy that he never betrayed a trace of
cynicism or moroseness, and that he never at any time of
crisis relaxed his efforts to influence directly and practically
the policy of his country. His whole life was illumined
by his vital faith in the Divine government of the world
and the Divine revelation which he saw in the history of
his people and experienced in his own consciousness. In
the practice and inculcation of that faith he never
wavered, and by its light he saw his own duty and that
of his countrymen, and read the lessons of history. At
every step of his career he exhibited the dominant
qualities of inflexible sincerity, moral earnestness, and
practical sagacity. The combination of these qualities
with the keenest spiritual insight, and a faith for which

the vision of God and His Kingdom was a living reality, gives the peculiar note of his greatness.

The most striking qualities of Isaiah's oratory are the force of its moral passion and its wealth of pointed imagery. Mention has already been made of his free use of illustrations drawn from the common scenes of rural life. Fire, flood, and storm furnish the material for lurid pictures of judgment and desolation. The portrayal of darkness and despair in the closing verses of ch. viii, of the irresistible progress of Assyrian conquest when towns were sacked as one might rifle a nest of its eggs, the birds too cowed to chirp (x. 14), of subtle moral deterioration ending in total ruin as a cracked wall bulges till it falls with a sudden crash (xxx. 13), of Yahwe as a lion, seizing Jerusalem, His prey, undismayed by the threats of the shepherds, its unworthy rulers (xxxi. 4), is the work of a master of imagery and of words. To the English reader some portions of Isaiah's discourses undoubtedly seem to be obscure. This apparent obscurity is largely due to the fact that the discourses, as we have them now before us, are isolated from the context of incident and circumstance which they presuppose. Reading them, therefore, in their present arrangement, one is apt to miss their point of attachment to actual circumstance, and thus to find them hard to follow. Placed, so far as it is now possible to place them, in their proper setting of historical back-ground, they are fine models of rapid, elevated, and forceful eloquence.

II. SOCIAL AND RELIGIOUS CONDITIONS IN THE TIME OF ISAIAH.

During the long reign of Uzziah (c. 780–740 B.C.) Judah made considerable progress in material prosperity. The government was strong, and order and security were well maintained. Trade flourished, wealth increased, and there was a rapid extension of intercourse with foreign

countries. The moral and economic results of these
changes were by no means wholly good, and what was
evil in them became apparent when the government
passed from the strong hands of Uzziah into those of his
weaker successors. The new wealth was unevenly dis-
tributed, so that class distinctions became more marked,
and while the rich grew richer, the poor tended to become
poorer. The small holdings of the peasant proprietors
were swallowed up by the larger estates (v. 8), and the
power of the purse was freely used to rob the poor by the
corruption of justice (i. 23 : v. 23 : x. 1 f.). A strongly
materialistic spirit pervaded the nation, which began to
glory in its newly acquired resources (ii. 7), and to resent
appeals to conscience based on purely moral and spiritual
ideas. These tendencies were checked to but a small
extent by the official religious teaching and observances.
The ceremonial aspects of religion were not neglected,
and its services were doubtless more splendidly conducted
than before owing to the increase of the national wealth
(ii. 11 ff.). But ceremonial observances were partly a matter
of habit, and partly a salve to conscience, and religion
ceased largely to be a real moral force in the lives of
the people. Alongside of the official worship of Yahwe
strange rites were practised. There were sacred trees and
wells (i. 29 ff.), there was open idolatry (ii. 8, 20), foreign
cults were introduced, such as that of Adonis (xvii. 10 f.,
referring to North Israel), while those inclined to darker
superstitions had recourse to magic arts and necromancy
(ii. 6 : viii. 19). These things were not new. There had
probably never been a time in the history of Israel when
the rich did not oppress the poor, when judges were not
corrupt, when idolatry and necromancy were not practised,
when moral exhortations and spiritual appeals did not fall
on deaf ears. It is clear, however, that Isaiah was convinced that the influx of wealth, the increase of luxury, and
the freer intercourse with foreign countries, that charac-

terised the middle decades of the eighth century, had
accentuated existing evils, and had produced a condition of
spiritual inertness and decay. That the prophet observed
accurately and judged rightly cannot be doubted. But it
should not be forgotten that he judged his contemporaries
by the severe standard of an awakened and purified
conscience. The social and religious conditions of
Isaiah's time, as he has portrayed them for us, were dark
enough, but it is partly the contrast between them and
the convictions and ideals of the prophetic conscience
which witnessed against them and condemned them, that
makes them seem darker than those of an earlier period.
On the other hand Isaiah's ministry was for his contemporaries a spiritual and ethical opportunity as well as
a test, and by disregarding it they condemned themselves.
The light was in their midst and they were blind to it.
For most of them Isaiah was what Elijah had been in the
eyes of Ahab, a troubler of Israel, and it was his insistence
on the ethical aspect of religion that troubled them. He
preached repentance, faith, and righteousness, and those
who contemptuously refused to listen to him (xxx. 11)
merited the severe condemnation which he passed upon
them. Their fundamental fault was not their rejection of
Isaiah's warnings or exhortations in regard to any
particular matter, but their total failure to grasp the first
principles of religion as Isaiah understood it, and as they
ought to have understood it. "God is a Spirit, and they
that worship Him must worship Him in spirit and in
truth" might well have been the motto of Isaiah's
ministry. Recognition of Yahwe's holiness, and of the
duties of obedience to His moral law and reliance on His
protection, was what Isaiah urged upon the people. A
self-reliant and self-seeking generation, with a materialistic view of life, and a materialistic conception of religion,
for the most part rejected his teaching, and was heedless
of his warnings.

III. ISAIAH'S PUBLIC CAREER IN ITS RELATION TO THE POLITICAL HISTORY OF HIS TIME.

The outstanding feature of the history of Western Asia in the latter half of the eighth century B.C. was the progress of Assyria as a conquering and absorbing power. The little Palestinian states and their neighbours were either completely subjugated or made tributary, and Egypt, though not actually invaded by an Assyrian army until the seventh century, was unable to offer any effective resistance to the westward progress of Assyrian conquest.

About the middle of the eighth century the kingdoms of Judah and Israel, under Uzziah and Jeroboam II respectively, were in a prosperous condition, but the successors of these strong kings were unable to maintain their independent position and resist Assyrian aggression. The northern kingdom fell into a state of almost anarchic confusion, a succession of kings reigning for brief periods, and falling victims in most cases to the conspiracies of ambitious rivals. In Judah Uzziah was succeeded, c. 740, by Jotham, whose reign, as sole ruler, lasted about four years. The reign of his son Ahaz began, c. 736, about the same time as that of Pekah in North Israel. Ahaz was succeeded, possibly in 727, though the date is far from certain, by his son Hezekiah, who was still on the throne in 701, the year of Sennacherib's invasion of Judah, and the last year to which any of Isaiah's prophecies may, with any considerable degree of probability, be assigned.

The Assyrian contemporaries of these kings were Tiglath-pileser III, 745–727 : Shalmaneser IV, 727–722 : Sargon, 722–705 : and Sennacherib, 705–681.

Under these vigorous rulers the Assyrian Empire was rapidly extended. In 738 Menahem of Israel paid tribute to Tiglath-pileser, and Assyria gained a permanent foothold in Palestine. A coalition of Pekah of Israel and

Rezin of Syria against Judah, c. 734, resulted in an appeal
by Ahaz for Assyrian assistance, and Tiglath-pileser,
nothing loth, subjugated Syria, Galilee, and Gilead,
capturing Damascus in 732, and receiving there the
homage of Ahaz, while Pekah was replaced on the throne
of Israel by Hoshea, at that time apparently a partisan of
Assyria. Shalmaneser invaded Israel on the defection of
Hoshea, and laid siege to Samaria, which fell shortly
after the accession of Sargon in 722. Sargon marched
past Judah in 720–19, and overthrew Gaza, near which, at
Raphia, he encountered and defeated an Egyptian army.
In 711 a revolt headed by Ashdod was crushed by the
Tartan, or commander-in-chief of the Assyrian army.
Ashdod was taken, but Judah, though sympathising with
the movement, saved itself by timely submission. The
death of Sargon in 705 encouraged the western states
tributary to Assyria to make a desperate effort to throw
off the yoke, and Egypt was ready with promises of
support. Sennacherib, Sargon's successor, was unable to
move westward till he had crushed a revolt in Babylonia
under Merodach-baladan, but in 701 he invaded Judah,
and laid it waste. He reduced Ekron, which had
dethroned Padi, his vassal, and defeated an Egyptian
army at Eltekeh. Jerusalem was blockaded, and Hezekiah
was forced to pay a heavy tribute, but the city was not
surrendered, and Sennacherib was compelled to proceed
southwards without attempting its capture by assault.
Having suffered a disaster not mentioned in his own
record of the campaign he returned to Assyria, and did
not again march into Palestine.

The career of Isaiah during these forty eventful years
may be divided, in accordance with the various changes
in the political situation of Judah, into four periods of very
unequal length :—

(a) *The early years*, 740–735 B.C.

The circumstances in which Isaiah entered upon his
prophetic ministry, and the emotions which his consciousness of a Divine call stirred within him, are recorded in
ch. vi. That chapter, therefore, though probably not
written till a few years after the event which it describes,
is the natural starting-point in a study of Isaiah's career.
The circumstances, to a man of Isaiah's character and
insight, were gloomy enough. Uzziah was dead, or dying,
and weaker hands were grasping the sceptre. North
Israel was in decay, and Judah, though still materially
prosperous, was in a state of moral deterioration due, in
great measure, to the luxury, selfishness, and ungodliness,
that material prosperity had engendered. The tide of
Assyrian conquest was creeping nearer year by year, and
to the illumined vision the shadow of coming judgment
lay dark on both the Hebrew kingdoms. Amid these
surroundings of political weakness and moral decay there
arose in the soul of Isaiah the vision of Yahwe, enthroned
in majesty and holiness, controlling the destinies alike of
His own unfaithful people and of the heathen empire, the
instrument of His wrath. He heard the Divine voice
summoning him to be an apostle to the people, and with
lips hot from contact with the cleansing fire of the Divine
holiness he offered himself in response to the call. It was
no light service that he undertook, nor did he undertake
it lightly. The preacher of repentance, righteousness,
faith, and judgment to come, had in that generation
an almost hopeless task, and Isaiah saw before him
a saddening prospect of calamities which he would be
powerless to avert. The course of events justified his
premonition, and practically throughout his life his chief
duty was to denounce and warn. Even when he heralds
the dawn of a new and brighter era, the dark night of
judgment must precede it.

In his earliest addresses—ch. ii–iv (with the possible exception of the idyllic passages, ii. 2–5: iv. 2–6, which may not be authentic): v. 1–24: and possibly also xxxii. 9–14—Isaiah dealt with the state of social and religious life in Judah. There was no political crisis, such as that which a few years later demanded his attention, and the country was as yet free from the political unrest which prevailed throughout his career from 735 onwards. Instead of this unrest, which at times passed into panic, there was ease, luxury, and self-confidence. This delusive security, the result of confidence in material resources, and this luxury, the product too often of fraud and injustice, Isaiah assailed with out-spoken vigour. On all sides, as he surveyed the condition of his country, he saw greed and selfishness, oppression and injustice, materialism, flagrant wickedness, and idolatry. Yahwe was forgotten, or remembered only in formal worship. Like Amos, Isaiah denounced these evils in unsparing language, and threatened his countrymen with an awful retribution. The Assyrian peril was not yet close at hand, and the Assyrians are not in these chapters explicitly designated as the instruments of the Divine wrath. But Isaiah was certain that the sins of the people would bring chastisement upon them, and as he watched the progress of Assyrian conquest he saw in it the sign of Yahwe's wrath, and the means by which His punitive judgment would be executed. In his next oracle[1]—ix. 8–x. 4 + v. 25–30—he described the wrath of Yahwe falling in successive blows on the northern kingdom, and in the closing verses of ch. v clearly indicated that the final blow in which the Divine wrath would work itself out on the impenitent people would be the invasion of Israel by an Assyrian army. Within a year or two a change in the political situation

---

[1] The word "oracle," as applied to Biblical writings (see Is. xiii. 1, R.V. marg.), means simply a discourse or utterance of a prophet.

brought the peril which threatened North Israel close to
the gates of Judah, and led Isaiah to address himself to
the problem of national policy.

(b) *The crisis of the Syro-Ephraimitic campaign,*
735–733 B.C.

The new feature in the political situation was the
alliance of Syria and North Israel against Judah.   In his
denunciation of North Israel, ix. 8–x. 4, v. 25–30, Isaiah
classed Syria among the open foes of the northern
kingdom (ix. 11 f.), an indication that mutual jealousy
had not yet given way to the common fear of Assyrian
invasion.   That fear, however, soon became the dominant
factor in the politics of Syria and Israel, and it became
the prime object of these peoples to effect a combination
strong enough to resist Assyrian aggression with some
hope of success.   An alliance was formed between Rezin
of Syria and Pekah of Israel, who determined to coerce
Judah into joining the league against Assyria.   With this
object in view they proposed to dethrone Ahaz, and set up
in his place a king of their own choosing (vii. 6).   The
allied armies marched against Judah, and struck terror
into the heart of Ahaz, who, in order to rid himself of the
immediate danger, proposed to ask help of Tiglath-pileser
of Assyria.   In spite of Isaiah's energetic protest this step
was taken, and Judah became, for practical purposes, a
vassal-state of Assyria, while the Syrian kingdom was
overthrown, and in Israel Pekah was put to death, and
Hoshea, his murderer, was placed upon the throne.   The
attitude of Isaiah at this juncture must be clearly understood, in view of his later exhortations to acquiescence in
the Assyrian suzerainty.   His view was that Syria and
Israel were doomed in any case, and that nothing could
save them.   Judah, on the other hand, had still a chance
of salvation through repentance and faith in Yahwe, who

would protect His people, if they returned to their spiritual allegiance and were faithful to Him. The policy of purchasing immediate deliverance from the pressure of the Syro-Ephraimitic coalition by submission to Assyria seemed to Isaiah to be an act at once of open disloyalty to Yahwe and of political suicide. Considering it from the spiritual point of view as a sin against Yahwe, concentrating in itself the people's refusal to repent and trust, and from the political point of view as an act of folly, he felt that it sealed the doom of Judah. Hence his strong protest against it.

His earliest reference to the new situation is to be found in xvii. 1-11, a denunciation of Syria and Israel, threatening them with total ruin. There is no reference to a concerted movement on the part of the allies against Judah, and it may be assumed that this part of their design was not yet ripe for action. Isaiah is concerned merely with the fate of the allied kingdoms, and especially with that of Israel, which had made an alliance with a heathen neighbour, and had sinned against Yahwe in adopting idolatrous customs, and in relying on material resources. Speedy destruction is threatened as the result of this short-sighted policy. Shortly after the publication of this oracle the allies invaded Judah (c. 734 B.C.), with the result already described. To this period of acute crisis belong ch. vii and viii. Isaiah had already (vii. 3) given expression to his belief that a small part of the nation would repent and form the nucleus of a regenerate people in the era subsequent to the Divine judgment, by naming one of his sons Shear-jashub, "a remnant shall turn." Now he endeavoured to save the nation by offering it the protection of Yahwe upon condition of repentance and faith. In an interview with Ahaz (vii. 3-17) he poured contempt upon the allies, and exhorted the king to trust Yahwe without fear, bidding him ask for a sign that might convince him that his

confidence would not be misplaced. The refusal of Ahaz
to ask for a sign was equivalent to a declaration that he
intended to adopt the policy of submission to Assyria,
and Isaiah thereupon predicted, in connection with the
sign of Immanuel, that the ruin of the allies would be
speedily followed by the desolation of Judah itself. The
remaining oracles of this period (vii. 18–viii) amplify the
warnings already conveyed in the interview with Ahaz,
and contain detailed predictions of the woe and desolation
which Assyrian invasion will bring upon Judah. By
giving a second son the symbolic name Maher-shalal-
hash-baz (viii. 3) Isaiah emphasised his threat of the
speedy fall of Damascus, to be followed by disaster to
Judah in consequence of the refusal of king and people to
trust Yahwe. At the same time he held fast the conviction
that no human power would be able to triumph over
Yahwe and those who were faithful to Him, and, undismayed by his failure to influence Ahaz, he gave
expression to his assurance of the ultimate victory of the
people of God (viii. 9 f.). The refusal, however, of Ahaz
and the mass of the people to listen to his reiterated
warnings—the language of vii. 13 suggests that he had
waged a long conflict with the court—led Isaiah to with-
draw for a time from public life, and to devote himself to
the instruction of his own disciples (viii. 16). To this
period of retreat we may plausibly assign the publication
of ch. vi, and perhaps also the collection and private
circulation among his disciples of Isaiah's early oracles.
The date of ch. i is uncertain, as the desolation of Judah
which it describes may have been the result either of the
Syro-Ephraimitic campaign in 734 or of Sennacherib's
invasion in 701. It may, however, not unreasonably be
assigned to the earlier period, and it may be regarded as
a compact exposition of the leading ideas of Isaiah's
preaching in the early years of his ministry.

*(c)   The period of formal acquiescence in the Assyrian
suzerainty,* 733–705 B.C.

For about 28 years after the recognition by Ahaz of
Tiglath-pileser's overlordship Judah refrained from actual
revolt against Assyria. This quiescence was in accordance with Isaiah's views, and was due, partly at least, to
his advice. His principle was that Judah should repent,
put its trust in Yahwe, and abstain from political and
military enterprises. From this point of view he had
opposed the policy of purchasing, by means of homage
and tribute, the assistance of Assyria against Syria and
Ephraim, and from the same point of view he now
opposed all adventurous schemes of revolt against the
galling yoke. He was convinced that the Assyrians were,
humanly speaking, irresistible, and that Yahwe alone
could deliver His people from them. His advice during
these years on the political question, which he could
never dissociate from the religious question, is summed
up in one of his later utterances, "In returning and rest
shall ye be saved ; in quietness and confidence shall be
your strength" (xxx. 15). At some date within this
period—the precise year is uncertain—Ahaz was succeeded
by Hezekiah, over whom Isaiah clearly exercised considerable influence. An increasingly powerful party,
however, at court and in the capital, persistently urged
the king to throw in his lot with the neighbouring states,
especially the Philistine cities, which aimed at deliverance
from the Assyrian bondage by concerted revolt in the
expectation of receiving decisive aid from Egypt. This
hope Isaiah regarded as wholly illusory. The pre-
dominance of the war party after 705 brought him into
violent and often bitter conflict with it, but up to that
date he seems to have been able to hold his own with the
king, and he was certainly successful in avoiding an open
rupture with Assyria.

The comparative success and serenity of the years 733–705 may perhaps account for the fact that there are hardly any extant memorials of Isaiah's activity during this whole period. The opening verses of ch. xxviii were certainly composed before the fall of Samaria in 722, but were republished in connection with a denunciation of the war party after 705. The oracle on Philistia, xiv. 28–32, which implies that an Assyrian king has just died (xiv. 29), may be assigned either to 727, the year in which Shalmaneser succeeded Tiglath-pileser, or to 722, when Sargon succeeded Shalmaneser, but it is at least equally probable that its true date is 705, the year of Sargon's death and Sennacherib's accession, and that it opens the last series of Isaiah's oracles. The Philistine envoys who solicit Judah's co-operation against Assyria are warned that revolt will only bring worse disaster upon them, while Judah is advised to decline their overtures and rely solely on the protection of Yahwe. The tone of the passage implies that Isaiah's influence was still supreme, and that the war party had not yet got the upper hand at court. Somewhat similar were the circumstances in 711, to which year the oracle on Egypt and Ethiopia, ch. xx, certainly belongs. The town of Ashdod had headed a revolt, with which Judah sympathised, and had appealed to Egypt for help. In 711 Sargon sent his Tartan, or commander-in-chief, to chastise the rebels. Ashdod was captured and looted, and its inhabitants were carried into captivity. As a warning to Judah against participation in the rising Isaiah went about for three years barefoot and without his outer garment. He was able to restrain Judah from open rebellion, and thus averted from it the chastisement which was meted out to Ashdod. It is evident from ch. xx that in 711 Isaiah anticipated further Assyrian conquests, and that the war party was already being restrained with difficulty from facing the risks of revolt in reliance on Egyptian assistance. Hezekiah himself chafed under the yoke of vassalage, and his reception of the embassy of Merodach-baladan (ch. xxxix), which may have been sent during this period (see note on xxxix. 1), shows that he was disposed to encourage the idea that he might join the ranks of the open foes of Assyria. While things were in this unsettled state, the war party in Judah agitating and intriguing, Hezekiah vacillating between caution and adventure, the Philistines eager as ever for another desperate attempt to regain their independence, and Egypt in the background encouraging the little Palestinian states to seize any favourable moment for revolt, an event happened which kindled the smouldering elements of disaffection into a blaze. Sargon, the mighty conqueror, died in 705, and was succeeded by Sennacherib. The favourable moment had come at last. From Babylonia to Philistia the subject states rose in revolt, and Judah was swept into the current. The remaining years of Isaiah's public life were largely spent in a great effort to restrain Judah from joining in the rebellion, and thus to avert the inevitable punishment at the hands of Assyria which rebellion would entail.

(d) *The Revolt from Assyria* 705-701 B.C.

It is not now possible to determine at what precise date Hezekiah yielded to the pressure of the war party, and committed himself definitely to the policy of revolt. In Isaiah's addresses criticism of the king is conspicuously absent, and the entire blame is thrown upon his advisers, who by intrigue and constant pressure forced his hand. We have seen how for some time after the accession of Sennacherib Isaiah's influence was dominant. This is still the case in ch. xviii (written between 705 and 702), which contains a firm and dignified answer by Isaiah to an Ethiopian embassy, which had been sent, as we may assume, with an offer of Ethiopian assistance to Hezekiah in the event of a rising against Assyria. Isaiah clearly expected that his advice would be followed, and the tone of the passage is markedly different from that of the scathing denunciations, xxviii–xxxi, delivered a little later. The most significant thought in ch. xviii is that Yahwe will intervene to destroy the Assyrians, and to exalt mount Zion, "the place of the name of Yahwe of Hosts." Isaiah had already, e.g. xiv. 32, expressed the confident belief that Judah, if faithful and trustful, would be secure under Divine protection, though the tide of Assyrian conquest would sweep over other states. Now, however, we encounter the idea that Yahwe has set a limit to Assyrian aggression, and that the destruction of the heathen empire by a signal manifestation of Divine power will inaugurate a new era of peace and righteousness under the rule of the Messianic king. This great idea appears in a group of prophecies, which may conveniently be considered together, their precise dates and relative order being uncertain. The group consists of ch. xviii : x. 5–34 : xiv. 24–27 : xvii. 12–14 : ix. 1–7 : xi. 1–9 : xxxii. 1–5, 15–20. In his early addresses Isaiah seems to anticipate a simple regeneration of the existing elements of society (e.g. i. 24–26). Later, however, he reached the conclusion that the regeneration could only be accomplished by means of a conspicuous and decisive manifestation of the Divine sovereignty in the establishment of a new and holy kingdom. At that decisive moment Assyria, so long invincible, would be defeated by Yahwe Himself, and the yoke lifted from the neck of the faithful people. At this stage Isaiah, still exercising a commanding influence in the counsels of his country, believed that repentance and faith might avert the extremity of disaster. He therefore spoke calmly and hopefully, as in ch. xviii, or almost exultingly, as in xiv. 24–27 : xvii. 12–14, which anticipate Yahwe's annihilation of the Assyrian hosts. The most elaborate oracle in the group is x. 5–34, which presents Isaiah's conception of Yahwe's relation to Assyria and to His own people. The Assyrians are His instruments for the chastisement of His people, but in their arrogance they ignore the Divine majesty, and propose to treat Yahwe as of no more account than a heathen idol. They will be allowed to march up to the gates of Jerusalem—an invasion of Judah was clearly in contemplation at the time, but not yet in actual progress, as the route described in x. 28-32 is not that of the actual line of attack followed by Sennacherib—but then, in their supreme moment of arrogant triumph, Yahwe will crush them, and will manifest His almighty power. The details of these anticipations cannot be pressed. Their dominant idea is the sovereignty of Yahwe, which will be made manifest in Zion, His chosen seat. The military movements of Assyria led almost inevitably to the feeling that the crisis was imminent, and that the end of the heathen domination was at hand. But as to the severity of the ordeal through which the people would pass, and the methods by which the deliverance would be wrought, there is no definiteness.

The same dominance of a central idea, and the same lack of consistent definiteness of detail are to be observed in the predictions relating to the Messianic kingdom, ix. 1-7 : xi. 1-9 : xxxii. 1-5. The dates of these passages are uncertain, and it is not even clear that they should all be assigned approximately to the same period of Isaiah's career, though they may conveniently be considered together.

The title Messiah ("anointed one") is never used by Isaiah, nor indeed in any part of the Old Testament, in the special sense of the expected deliverer and king. The passages under consideration are called Messianic because they depict an ideal community ruled by God Himself through the king, His representative on earth. It is not clear that Isaiah expected the future king to be the deliverer of his people from the Assyrian yoke. The deliverance is to be wrought rather by the unmediated intervention of Yahwe Himself. Nor is it clear that the attributes and functions of the Messianic king were regarded by Isaiah as belonging exclusively to one individual rather than to a succession of righteous kings, of whom the first, the inaugurator of the new era and of the new ideal of kingship, was the type. From ix. 6 it may be gathered that Isaiah's hopes centred in a royal child to be born after the Divine interposition and deliverance, the first offspring and future hero of the new and regenerate age. Generally speaking, however, the personality of the king is not more prominent in these Messianic forecasts than it must inevitably be in a monarchic constitution. Isaiah is not concerned with the external features of the constitution of the Divine kingdom, but with the spirit which will animate king, nobles, and people, a spirit of faith, obedience, holiness, and righteousness, and, in the case of those who bear rule, a spirit also of wisdom, justice, and power. The characteristic of the kingdom is the perfect realisation of the Divine sovereignty and holiness. Isaiah's conception of Yahwe as sovereign and as holy was the basis of his conviction that retribution would fall on the unfaithful people, that the heathen domination would be ended as soon as its continuance became an insult to Yahwe and a menace to His ideal kingdom, and that the ideal kingdom would be realised on earth. These convictions, in one form or another, pervaded his teaching throughout his career, and at no period were they clearer and stronger than when, just before the final crisis, he published the oracle on Assyria, x. 5–34.

We now come to the last phase of Isaiah's public ministry, the actual crisis of revolt and invasion, 702–01 B.C. The discourses of this period, ch. xxii : xxviii–xxxi, show that it was a time of storm and stress, of strenuous and even acrimonious conflict. The war party had gained the upper hand at court and with the people, and Isaiah clearly felt that, humanly speaking, he was fighting a losing battle. After a vain attempt to conceal their project from the prophet (xxix. 15), the party in power entered openly into alliance with Egypt, with a view especially to supplementing their meagre strength in the cavalry arm (xxxi. 1). Against this alliance, with all that it involved of confidence in material resources and mistrust of Yahwe, as well as of appalling risk of invasion and loss, Isaiah contended with all the strength that was in him. The precise sequence of events during this crisis is uncertain, and the mingling of threat and promise in Isaiah's discourses, xxviii–xxxi, renders them somewhat obscure. At first sight the minatory passages appear to be irreconcilable with the promises of deliverance, and it seems hardly credible that they should both have emanated from the same mind at about the same period. The question is whether we can find a guiding-thread which, without necessarily explaining all the difficulties, may render Isaiah's general attitude intelligible. We have seen that he cherished the conviction that Yahwe would interpose His almighty power to deliver the faithful among His people, and to establish His kingdom in righteousness. How far, then, did the unbelief and unfitness for the Messianic kingdom exhibited anew by the rulers of the people in the formation of the Egyptian alliance materially alter the situation? Their action increased tenfold the peril of Judah; it was certain to entail a heavy punishment; and it destroyed their own chance of participating in the deliverance and in the blessedness of the new era. But it could not render nugatory, though it might impede or modify, the purposes of Yahwe. Through the disobedience of its rulers Jerusalem had become an altar-hearth ("Ariel" xxix. 1 f.), a place of slaughter. Yahwe would fight against it, and take it from those unworthy to hold it, as a lion seizes its prey, a sheep from the flock, undismayed by the menaces of the shepherds (xxxi. 4). But the faithful remnant remained, and the Divine purpose stood firm. The

Assyrians would be no more able than before to obstruct the establishment of the holy kingdom, though the chastisement inflicted through their instrumentality might be more severe. That the thought of Isaiah followed some such course as this is probable in view of his teaching before the crisis, and of the contents of his addresses during the crisis. That ch. xxviii–xxxi have suffered interpolation is highly probable. But the excision of all the promises from these chapters on the *a priori* ground that Isaiah made no such promises is an arbitrary proceeding. This view is confirmed by xxviii. 23-29, which is, in effect, the prophet's defence of himself against the charge of inconsistency to which the mingling of threat and promise in his addresses not unnaturally gave rise. In the discourses of this period, therefore, we have echoes of Isaiah's conflict with the dominant party, of his denunciations of them and of their policy, of his efforts to save his country from its impending fate, and his threats of siege, slaughter, and desolation ; and also of his imperishable faith in the ultimate triumph of Yahwe over both His own unfaithful people and the heathen empire.

Probably the earliest passage in the chapters under consideration is xxii. 15-25, or as much of it as is genuine. In this passage Isaiah attacks Shebna, apparently a foreign adventurer, who, it may be assumed, was a leader of the war party. The attack was at least partially successful, and Shebna lost his high office, though, if xxxvi. 3 be accurate, he was not dismissed altogether from the king's service. The tone of the invective against Shebna indicates that the tension between Isaiah and those opposed to him was becoming unbearably acute, and that the prophet was being roused to a supreme effort by the waning of his influence. Still more menacing is the tone of xxviii. 1-22, in which the prophet exposes the sensuality, irreligion, and political folly of the now dominant war party, and denounces judgment upon the disobedient people, pointing the threat by the republication of an oracle on Samaria (*vv.* 1–4), where similar vices had led to overwhelming disaster. In ch. xxix we have the first hint of the Egyptian alliance, which was still apparently an official secret (*v.* 15), and further denunciations mingled with predictions of future deliverance, of which the authenticity is in some cases very doubtful. The arrangement of the discourses in these chapters is hardly chronological, but proceeds rather from the editorial desire to attach the promises of deliverance and grace as closely as possible to the threats of wrath and judgment. Ch. xxx and xxxi contain echoes of the agitated movements of the time, of the high hopes built on the Egyptian alliance, of an embassy carrying rich presents to the ally across the desert to the south, of the thunders of Isaiah's invective against the war policy, his outbursts of wrath, and his triumphant declarations that Yahwe would still conquer and reign in spite of all. At some dark moment during the crisis, possibly when the attitude of the people after Sennacherib's retreat had revealed how little they had profited by warning, chastisement, and grace, Isaiah gave utterance to the sombre forebodings of xxii. 1–14, in which he declares that the people's sin is inexpiable, and in the name of Yahwe pronounces sentence of death upon them.

These vivid chapters unfortunately contain no explicit statements as to the negotiations between Sennacherib and Hezekiah, or the efforts of Sennacherib to effect the reduction of Jerusalem, or the cause of his return to Assyria. From the Assyrian record of the campaign, and from II Kings xviii. 13–16, we learn that Hezekiah endeavoured to purchase immunity from assault and destruction by the payment of a heavy tribute. In Is. xxxvi, xxxvii (= II Kings xviii. 17—xix. 37) we have the Hebrew traditions respecting the negotiations with Sennacherib's representative, the Rab-shakeh, and the

causes of Sennacherib's retreat. On these points the
Assyrian record is silent. It may reasonably be assumed,
however, that this silence conceals a disaster which was
the cause of Sennacherib's sudden return to Assyria, and
that the Hebrew narratives, though undoubtedly obscure,
and probably inaccurate on points of detail, are based on
an authentic tradition.

How long Isaiah survived this great crisis in his
country's history we do not know. So far as we are able
to judge from his extant writings his public activity ceased
with the withdrawal of the Assyrian invader, an event
which closed a great chapter in the history of Judah. He
bequeathed to his disciples and to mankind the memory
of a noble life spent consistently and unselfishly in the
service of God and of man, the inalienable inheritance of
his great spiritual ideas, and the inspiration of his faith
and hope.

IV. ISAIAH'S FUNDAMENTAL CONCEPTIONS.

The great principles and ideas characteristic of Isaiah's
teaching have been brought out in the course of the
preceding sections, and it is not necessary to do more
than summarise them here.

Isaiah was not the first of the prophets, and his teaching,
as far as its main outlines were concerned, was not new.
The Divine sovereignty and holiness, the special duty of
Israel, the chosen people, to Yahwe, the certainty of an
awful retribution for the unbelief, disobedience, and un-
righteousness of the people, and the futility of resistance,
based on reliance on human resources, to Assyria, the
Divine instrument for the chastisement of Israel, had
already been emphasised and set clearly before the people
of the northern kingdom by Amos and Hosea, and the
same ideas form the basis of Isaiah's teaching. Hosea's
special contribution to prophetic teaching—the thought of

the yearning love of Yahwe for His people in spite of its unfaithfulness and disobedience, and of the answering love owed by the people—hardly appears in the discourses of Isaiah, whose conception of the Divine authority and of the people's duty is more austere, and recalls rather that of Amos. All these prophets, however, as well as Micah, the other great religious teacher of the eighth century, build upon the same fundamental ideas. Isaiah is distinguished from the other prophets by the fact that he was a statesman as well as a teacher, a man of action as well as a thinker. He applied his principles and ideas to urgent political problems, and even his visions of the ideal future, though dominated by a great spiritual conception, have a practical and political cast. Breadth of view and precision of detail are perhaps the chief qualities which distinguish his handling of the common fundamental ideas of the prophetic teaching.

The great conceptions underlying Isaiah's teaching may be arranged in three main divisions :—i. The conception of Yahwe. ii. The conception of Israel's duty to Yahwe. iii. Eschatological conceptions.

i. *Isaiah's conception of Yahwe.*

(*a*) *The majesty and universal sovereignty of Yahwe.* For Isaiah Yahwe was the one God, the only ruler of men and disposer of events. The chant of the seraphim, "The whole earth is full of His glory," had sounded in his ears at the beginning of his ministry, and the idea of Yahwe, reigning in solitary and unapproachable majesty, lay at the root of all his thinking and teaching. Like Amos, Isaiah regarded all nations as equally under Yahwe's sway. The gods of the heathen were nonentities, "nothings," as he contemptuously calls them. The heathen nations fulfilled their destiny in the Divine plan, and though they failed to recognise Yahwe, they were nevertheless, in their political relations, wholly under His control, to be employed, if He had a use for them, as instruments for the execution of His purposes. The forces of nature manifested the Divine power and majesty. The course of human history was the unfolding of the Divine purpose. Of that purpose the essential and commanding feature was the establishment of Yahwe's kingdom, the acknowledgment by mankind of His majesty and His spiritual sovereignty.

(*b*) *Yahwe's holiness.* The first word, thrice repeated, of the seraphic chant, "Holy, holy, holy, is Yahwe of Hosts," struck the keynote of Isaiah's ethical conception of the Divine nature and sovereignty. The word "holy" had at first no ethical connotation, and emphasised the separateness of the Divine Being, as something apart from all other forms of existence, rather than any specially ethical attribute of the Divine nature. As used by the prophets, however, the word came to connote all that separated Yahwe, not only from nature and man, but from the heathen deities, from whom He was distinguished by His ethical character as well as by His unique majesty. Holiness was thus the essential attribute of Yahwe, a quality peculiarly His own, embracing His unapproachable exaltation, His abhorrence of all that was untrue, unclean, or sinful, and His eternal righteousness.

(*c*) *Yahwe, the God of Israel.* Yahwe's special relation to Israel was in no sense a limitation of His universal sovereignty ; it was rather a particular manifestation of it, a step towards the full exhibition and realisation of it upon earth. It consisted in His choice of a single people to be the recipients of His revelation of His nature and will, and the immediate sphere of His kingly rule. The revelation was made partly through individuals—Isaiah was vividly conscious of his own responsibility as the bearer of a Divine message—and partly through the history of the nation. Yahwe had let Israel know Him, He had given Israel every advantage (i. 2 : v. 1 ff.). He had made Zion the chosen seat of His Divine kingdom. Israel was His people, and He was, in a special sense, Israel's God. It should be observed that for Isaiah, as for the other prophets of his time, the nation is the religious unit, not the individual soul. The prophets contemplated with awe the stupendous fact that the God of all the earth had entered into this special relation to their own people. To the people as a whole they spoke in the name of God, recalling the nation to a sense of its privilege and its duty. Isaiah had no sympathy with the vulgar national pride of his countrymen in their God, a pride that was hardly to be distinguished from that of the heathen in their false deities. But he gloried in Yahwe's relation to Israel as a special manifestation of His sovereignty and holiness. His favourite designation of Yahwe, "The Holy One of Israel," a phrase of which his countrymen grew weary (xxx. 11), gives expression to his sense not only of the ethical character of the Divine relation to Israel, but also of the supreme spiritual value of the Divine revelation vouchsafed to Israel.

ii. *Isaiah's conception of Israel's duty to Yahwe.*

As Yahwe had revealed Himself primarily to Israel, it was to Israel that He looked for recognition, knowledge, and obedience (i. 2 ff.: v. 1 ff.). His universal sovereignty was mirrored in His kingship over Israel, and Israel was therefore under a special obligation to Him. The nation's duty, as Isaiah conceived it, was, in general, to obey the Divine revelation, and reflect the Divine character. More particularly, it might be summed up under three heads : (*a*) repentance, (*b*) service, (*c*) faith.

(*a*) *Repentance.* The fundamental fault of the people was that they did not realise the holiness of Yahwe, that they did not understand the nature and significance of the high privilege He had conferred upon them, nor the duty

which He required of them. All the particular vices
which Isaiah denounced had their root in this fundamental
spiritual failure. " Israel doth not know, my people doth
not consider" (i. 5). Their idolatry, their reliance on
material resources, their greed, selfishness, injustice, and
sensuality, their religious formalism, and their indifference
to the Divine message delivered by the prophet, were all
evidence of a deep-seated uncleanness, ungodliness, and
apostasy. Their first duty was to turn to God, to abandon
their fundamentally wrong attitude to Him, and make a
new beginning in a right relation to Him. A striking,
and indeed startling, feature of Isaiah's ministry was
his conviction that the spiritual incapacity of the people
was so deep-seated and complete that his message would
fall on deaf ears, and that the light of truth that shone
through him would but intensify the surrounding darkness.
This conviction did not relieve him of the duty of preaching
repentance. Nor did it deprive him altogether of the hope
that a part of the nation would repent, and would form
the seed of a holy people. It accentuated, however, the
austerity of his warnings and denunciations. He set
before the people, not in tones of tender pleading, but
with the accent of authority, the prime necessity of a
total change in their attitude to God.

(*b*) *Service*. Isaiah's conception of the Divine sovereignty and holiness led inevitably to the conviction that
the only acceptable service of God was obedience to
His sovereign and holy will. Throughout his preaching
therefore, Isaiah emphasised, with what seemed to his
countrymen to be monotonous reiteration (xxviii. 10), the
ethical aspect of religion. " Cease to do evil, learn to do
well" (i. 17) was the burden of his message. Merely
formal recognition of Yahwe he denounced as useless,
and elaborate ritual, unaccompanied by hearty obedience
and righteous conduct, was in his eyes futile and even
blasphemous (i. 10–17). The true service of God was not

formal worship, but sincerity and justice, purity and mercy. The ethical ideal, to which the people were blind, was the standard by which they must be judged.

(c) *Faith.* In his interview with Ahaz (vii. 3 ff.) Isaiah laid down the principle that the national security depended upon the people's faith (vii. 9). The same principle is inculcated in his later discourses (xxviii. 16: xxx. 15), and must be regarded as a cardinal feature of his teaching. Faith meant willingness to follow the Divine guidance, to obey the Divine will, and to rely on the Divine protection. Yahwe was not an unknown God. He had revealed Himself to His people, and He was still revealing His will and purpose through His prophets. Isaiah had heard the Divine voice in his own soul, and his assurance of the almighty power and ultimate triumph of Yahwe was clear and steadfast. In Yahwe's name he promised king and people the Divine protection upon condition of obedience and trust. Implicit confidence in Yahwe's guidance and sovereign power was the mainspring of his own religious life, and he demanded of the people that they should accept and obey the Divine message with which he felt himself to be charged. It is little wonder that the statesmen of his time, busied with their schemes of diplomacy and military defence, could not follow him to the lofty height of faith on which he himself stood firm.

iii. *Eschatological conceptions.*

Isaiah's eschatology is not concerned with the last things of an entirely remote future, but with events which seemed to him to be impending. His predictions of these events are not apocalyptic, not a lifting of the veil which hides the distant future from human eyes, but are rather the direct consequence of his ethical conception of Yahwe's nature and purposes. He saw with awful clearness of vision the sin and spiritual darkness of the

people ; and, like the other prophets of the age, he threatened them, in Yahwe's name, with a drastic retribution.
Persistent wickedness and unfaithfulness must result in
the desolation of the land and the destruction of the
people. To Isaiah, as to Amos, the " Day of Yahwe "
(ii. 12 : Amos v. 18), to which the people looked forward
as a day of deliverance and vengeance, was a day of wrath
and judgment upon Israel. In that day Yahwe would
destroy all that was opposed to His will, all that infringed
upon His sovereign rights. Would that involve the
destruction of the whole people ? Sometimes Isaiah
speaks as if he saw no light beyond the gloom, and
in his early prophecies especially he uses the most uncompromising terms in depicting the impending judgment. Yet the doom of that generation could not stultify
the Divine purpose, and almost at the beginning of his
ministry Isaiah gave expression, in the name Shear-jashub
(vii. 3), to his faith that a remnant of the people would
turn to God, and that this remnant, which would survive
the judgment, would be the seed of a new and holy nation.
The idea of a faithful remnant is the germ of the conception of the ideal Israel, a holy and indestructible people,
existing in spite of the infidelity of any particular
generation. As the years passed the idea of the salvation
of the Remnant took more complete hold of Isaiah's
mind, and the future kingdom of God shaped itself with
more precision of detail before the eye of faith. The
" Day of Yahwe " became a day not only of judgment
upon the unfaithful people, but also of destruction for the
heathen foe, and of deliverance for the faithful. The
actual Israel would perish, but the ideal Israel would
be redeemed and restored. The Assyrian, so long
the instrument of Yahwe's wrath, would be crushed
when his chastising work was done, and Yahwe would
reign supreme on Zion, His chosen seat. Thus alongside
of portrayals of the destruction to be wrought on an

impenitent and ungodly Israel we have visions of the discomfiture of the heathen, and of the establishment of the Divine kingdom. In his earlier years Isaiah had contemplated a prolonged desolation of the land, and had even hinted that the Divine chastisement might take the form of a captivity of the people (v. 13), as Amos and Hosea had predicted. In the later discourses, however, the two aspects of the impending judgment—the chastisement of Israel, and the destruction of the heathen power —are blended together in such a way as to create the impression that Isaiah anticipated a single decisive act of Yahwe, which would overwhelm the existing Israel, annihilate the heathen invader, and inaugurate the new era. In that new and glorious era Yahwe would reign in righteousness, through the king, His earthly representative, over a holy and God-fearing people. The leading features of Isaiah's forecasts of the Messianic kingdom have already been described. The point that requires to be emphasised is that these anticipations were the fruit of the great central conception of the holiness and universal sovereignty of Yahwe. A seer, who was also a statesman, translated his ideal into an actual polity, and depicted a king, endowed with the spirit of God, supported by a purified and truly noble aristocracy, ruling in peace and righteousness over a regenerate people.

V. The present arrangement and probable composition of Isaiah i–xxxix.

Isaiah i–xxxix, as at present arranged, may be divided into five sections:

   (i) i–xii. Prophecies relating chiefly to Judah.

   (ii) xiii–xxiii. A series of prophecies relating chiefly to foreign nations.

   (iii) xxiv–xxvii. The Divine judgment on the world, and the salvation of Israel.

These chapters contain the extant discourses of Isaiah, and also a considerable number of anonymous prophecies, written, for the most part, long after Isaiah's time.   In general it may be said that Isaiah's prophecies were first delivered in public, and were subsequently written down by himself or his disciples.   Various separate discourses were then collected together into a roll or volume (viii. 16 : cf. Jer. xxxvi. 1–8), to which fresh material might from time to time be added.   In process of time, as these rolls were handed down from generation to generation, and copied, and rearranged, anonymous prophecies were attached to them, and ultimately the several collections were combined together to form a single volume.   We are not dealing, therefore, with a single book issued at a particular time, but with a series of collections of separate prophecies, and with a protracted process of arranging and editing, which began when Isaiah collected his early utterances for circulation among his disciples (viii. 16), and did not end until the book that bears his name assumed its present form at some date long after the exile.   The details of the process are obscure, but its general outlines are fairly clear.   There were three volumes, or collections, of Isaianic oracles (groups i, ii, iv above), to which anonymous prophecies were added from time to time until the volumes assumed their present form.   The apocalyptic prophecy, section iii, may have been attached to ii before the final amalgamation of the several collections into a single volume was effected, or it may have existed independently until that time.   If the former alternative be preferred, the last stage in the process of compiling and editing i–xxxix, apart from possible slight additions or rearrangements, was the publication in a single volume of the three collections, i–xii, xiii–xxvii, xxviii–xxxv, along with the historical appendix, xxxvi–xxxix.

i. The first collection, i–xii, consists for the most part of Isaiah's early discourses (ii–viii, ix. 8–x. 4, and possibly also i), along with one or two which belong to a later period of his career (x. 5–34, and probably also ix. 1–7, xi. 1–9, and some anonymous passages (xi. 10–xii, and perhaps ii. 2–5, iv. 2–6).

The title of the collection (i. 1) states that it comprises prophecies relating to Judah and Jerusalem, thus distinguishing it from the volume containing oracles on foreign nations. It may be assumed that the basis of the collection was Isaiah's own edition of his early prophecies (viii. 16), to which fresh material was added, perhaps by Isaiah himself, up to the date of the cycle of discourses on Judaean politics (xxviii–xxxi), which formed a distinct group. The late Isaianic passages in the first collection, such as x. 5–34, and i, if it be assigned to the later period, are distinguished from this group by their more general character, and may also be slightly earlier in date.

The arrangement of the prophecies in the volume is not chronological. Ch. i owes its position doubtless to the general and comprehensive character of its contents, and not to its date, while ix. 8–x. 4, v. 25–30 is almost certainly earlier than vii f. The general principle of the arrangement is that words of consolation and hope should be placed after each denunciatory or minatory passage, so that threat and promise succeed each other in almost regular alternation. The volume closes with a lyric epilogue (ch. xii), suitable for liturgical use in the post-exilic community. The present arrangement of the book, from the formal superscription to the liturgical close, shows that it was at one time a separate volume, complete in

itself, and further that its editors had in view its devotional
use, rather than chronological or historical considerations.

ii. The second group, xiii–xxiii, consists chiefly of
miscellaneous oracles on foreign nations. It is a series
of detached pieces, most of which bear the editorial title
"massa" (R. V. marg. "oracle"). The Isaianic basis of
the group comprises xiv. 28–32 (Philistia), xvii. 1–11
(Damascus and Ephraim), xviii (Ethiopia), and xx
(Ashdod, Egypt, and Ethiopia), along with xiv. 24–27 and
xvii. 12–14, two fragments anticipating Yahwe's deliverance of His people from the heathen oppression, and xxii,
which seems somewhat out of place in this volume.

Round this nucleus of Isaianic prophecy were gathered
various anonymous oracles on foreign nations. The
oracle on Moab, xv, xvi, may be the work of an earlier
prophet than Isaiah, who may have republished it with an
addition of his own (xvi. 13 f.). The oracles on Egypt,
xix, and Phoenicia, xxiii, may also be Isaiah's, though
their authenticity is extremely doubtful, and their date
quite uncertain. On the other hand xiii. 2–xiv. 23 and
xxi contain anticipations of the impending fall of Babylon,
and are both to be assigned to the later years of the exile,
though they differ too widely in style and point of view to
be ascribed to the same author.

iii. The third section of the book, xxiv–xxvii, is entirely post-exilic. Though composite in structure, it now
forms a single connected piece, which probably existed in
its present arrangement before its combination with the
rest of the book. Its subject—the Divine judgment on
the world, and the deliverance of Israel—makes it a not
unsuitable conclusion to the collection of oracles on
foreign nations, to which it may have been attached
before the combination of the several volumes into a
single book.

iv. The fourth section, xxviii–xxxv, comprises the third
collection of Isaiah's prophecies, with the addition of one

or more anonymous pieces. In xxviii–xxxi we have a compact series of discourses on the politics of Judah at the crisis of the Egyptian alliance and the invasion of Sennacherib, and xxxii may perhaps belong approximately to the same period. These discourses, though doubtless subsequently edited and rearranged, may well have been collected and published by Isaiah himself, and there may be a hint of this in xxx. 8. The authenticity and date of xxxiii are very doubtful, while the last oracle in the collection, xxxiv, xxxv, depicting the Divine judgment on the world, especially on Edom, and the blessedness of the redeemed Israel, is certainly post-exilic. It bears a considerable resemblance to xxiv–xxvii, and its position at the close of this volume lends some support to the idea that xxiv–xxvii formed the conclusion of the second volume before the final amalgamation.

Thus each of the three collections, in their final arrangement, closes on a note of joyful and buoyant hope.

v. The historical appendix, xxxvi–xxxix, consists in the main of extracts from II Kings, describing three incidents in the reign of Hezekiah, in which Isaiah figures prominently. The editor has abbreviated the text of II Kings, and has added Hezekiah's psalm of thanksgiving on his recovery, xxxviii. 10–20. Whether this section existed independently in its present form before the amalgamation of i–xxxv into a single volume cannot be determined. It may be that it was compiled for the first time when the whole book was issued. In any case its purpose is sufficiently clear. The editor had in view the convenience of readers of the book of Isaiah who might be glad to have, in one volume, all that was known of the prophet's life and work.

VI. THE CONTENTS OF THE BOOK ARRANGED IN THEIR PROBABLE CHRONOLOGICAL ORDER.

A. The prophecies of Isaiah.

(1) The early period, 740–735 B.C.
ii–iv, except possibly the lyric passages (ii. 2–5 : iv. 2–6).
v. 1–24.
ix. 8–x. 4, v. 25–30.
xxxii. 9–14 (? or 701).

(2) The crisis of the Syro-Ephraimitic invasion, 735–733 B.C.
xvii. 1–11.
vii, viii.
vi.
i (? or 701).

(3) The period of formal acquiescence in the Assyrian suzerainty, 733–705 B.C.
xxviii. 1–4 (before the fall of Samaria, 722/1, subsequently republished in 702/1).
xx (711).

(4) The crisis of the Egyptian alliance, and the revolt against Assyria, 705–701 B.C.
xiv. 28–32 (705 : ? or 727, or 722).
x. 5–34 : xiv. 24–27 : xvii. 12–14 : ix. 1–7 : xi. 1–9 : xxxii. 1–8, 15–20 (?).
xviii.
xxii. 15 ff.
xxviii–xxxi.
xxii. 1–14.

(5) Of doubtful authenticity and uncertain date, probably post-exilic.
xix, xxiii, xxxiii.

B. Anonymous prophecies.

(1) Possibly pre-exilic.
  ii. 2–4 : xv, xvi.

(2) Exilic.
  xiii. 2–xiv. 23 : xxi.

(3) Post-exilic, of uncertain date.
  (*a*) xxiv–xxvii.
  (*b*) xi. 10–xii : xxxiv, xxxv.
  (*c*) Probably xix : xxiii : xxxiii.
  (*d*) The compilation of xxxvi–xxxix.

Literature. For the sake of brevity references to authorities have been excluded from the notes in this volume, in the preparation of which the following works have been consulted.

English commentaries :—Cheyne ; G. A. Smith (*Expositor's Bible*) ; Skinner (*Cambridge Bible*): Whitehouse (*Century Bible*).

German commentaries :—Dillmann, revised by Kittel ; Duhm ; Marti.

Other works :—Cheyne, *Introduction to the book of Isaiah* ; W. R. Smith, *The Prophets of Israel* ; Driver, *Isaiah, his Life and Times* ; Smend, *Alttestamentliche Religionsgeschichte* ; and the relevant articles in the *Encyclopaedia Biblica*, and in Hastings' *Dictionary of the Bible.*

ISAIAH

i. *Yahwe and Israel: sin, judgment, and restoration.*

THE vision of Isaiah the son of Amoz, which he saw **1** concerning Judah and Jerusalem, in the days of Uzziah, Jotham, Ahaz, and Hezekiah, kings of Judah.

Hear, O heavens, and give ear, O earth, for the LORD **2**

Ch. i.–xii. A COLLECTION OF PROPHECIES RELATING CHIEFLY TO JUDAH AND ISRAEL.

I. Ch. i.

The passage is general and comprehensive, and strikes the fundamental notes of Isaiah's teaching. To these features it probably owes its introductory position. It contains no specific indication of date, as the description of the desolation of the land under invasion might fairly apply either to the Syro-Ephraimitish war in 735 B.C., or to the campaign of Sennacherib in 701; while the internal disorders of the state, though more pronounced under Ahaz than under Hezekiah, doubtless existed throughout Isaiah's life. The fresh and vigorous tone of the passage, and its resemblance to other early work of Isaiah (e.g. ch. ii.–iv.), may, in the absence of any determining evidence, justify a preference for the earlier date.

i. 1. Editorial superscription to ch. i.–xii.

The wide range of time indicated by ' in the days...Judah,' covering the whole of Isaiah's public life, shows that this is the title, not of a single prophecy, but of an entire volume. On the other hand, the words 'concerning Judah and Jerusalem' limit its scope to ch. i.–xii.

vision: what the seer saw with the eye of the spirit; what he learned in communion with God: hence used in the sense of his message, or the revelation of God through him, and later as the general title of a collection of prophecies, as here; cf. Nah. i. 1; Ob. 1.

2, 3. Yahwe's complaint against His people.

The emphasis is on the filial relationship between Yahwe and His people, who are ignorant, disobedient, and ungrateful.

hath spoken : I have nourished and brought up children,
3 and they have rebelled against me.   The ox knoweth his
owner, and the ass his master's crib : *but* Israel doth
4 not know, my people doth not consider.   Ah sinful
nation, a people laden with iniquity, a seed of evil-doers,
children that deal corruptly : they have forsaken the
LORD, they have despised the Holy One of Israel, they
5 are estranged *and gone* backward.   Why will ye be still
stricken, that ye revolt more and more? the whole head
6 is sick, and the whole heart faint.   From the sole of the
foot even unto the head there is no soundness in it; *but*
wounds, and bruises, and festering sores : they have not
been closed, neither bound up, neither mollified with oil.
7 Your country is desolate ; your cities are burned with
fire ; your land, strangers devour it in your presence, and
8 it is desolate, as overthrown by strangers.   And the
daughter of Zion is left as a booth in a vineyard, as a
lodge in a garden of cucumbers, as a besieged city.

---

nourished and brought up.   The reference is chiefly to the
spiritual gifts, to the source and value of which they were blind ;
cf. Hosea ii. 5-8.

4-9.   The prophet enlarges and emphasizes Yahwe's complaint.

5.   Why ?   Another rendering is ' where—on what part—can
another blow fall ? ' the whole body being already wounded and
diseased.

7.   Metaphor gives place to vivid description.

strangers : the Assyrians, if the passage refer to Sennacherib's
invasion in 701 : or Syrians, with whom the northern Israelites
were allied, if the reference be to the campaign of 735.   The
word ' foreigners ' is not decisive against the latter view.

desolate...strangers : lit. ' a desolation like an overthrow of
[or by] strangers.'   The sense is weak, as the simile of pillage to
describe pillage lacks point.   Read ' like the overthrow of
Sodom,' an emendation supported by the constant association
of the word for ' overthrow ' with Sodom (cf. Deut. xxix. 23 ;
Jer. xlix. 18), and by the reference in *v.* 9.

8.   A picture of loneliness and isolation.   The daughter, Zion
(a poetical personification of the city), stands alone in the midst
of a desolate country, like a night-watchman's rough shelter, a

Except the LORD of hosts had left unto us a very small 9
remnant, we should have been as Sodom, we should have
been like unto Gomorrah.

Hear the word of the LORD, ye rulers of Sodom; give 10
ear unto the law of our God, ye people of Gomorrah.
To what purpose is the multitude of your sacrifices unto 11
me? saith the LORD: I am full of the burnt offerings of
rams, and the fat of fed beasts; and I delight not in the
blood of bullocks, or of lambs, or of he-goats. When ye 12
come to appear before me, who hath required this at your

booth or cabin, in the open fields. **As a besieged city**
expresses the idea of isolation under another image, but the exact
meaning is doubtful: lit. 'a watched city.'

9. the Lord of hosts: 'Yahwe (God) of Hosts,' a title of
doubtful origin, possibly meaning in the first instance 'God of
the armies of Israel' (cf. for the idea 1 Sam. xvii. 45), but used
by the prophets in an extended sense to denote Yahwe's
command of all the forces of nature, and all the powers of men.
Another view connects the phrase with the 'host of Heaven'
(angels, or stars); cf. 1 Kings xxii. 19; Ps. cxlviii. 2, 3. In any
case its use by the prophets emphasizes the all-embracing sovereignty of Yahwe (cf. LXX Παντοκράτωρ).

10-17. The true service of God—not ceremonial observance,
but obedience to the moral law.

10. The reference to the destruction of Sodom, *v.* 9, suggests
a moral resemblance between the 'rulers' (strictly 'judges')
of Sodom and those of Jerusalem.

law: parallel to 'word,' and with practically the same
meaning. 'Torah'—law—meant originally a specific answer
by the priest to a question affecting ritual or conduct, or
a declaration by priest or prophet of the will of God in a
particular case. Subsequently the word was used for religious
instruction, especially that of the prophets speaking in the name
of God, as here. Still later it was applied as a technical term
to the codified law, and then to the Pentateuch, in which the
law was embodied.

11. I am full of...: i.e. 'I am sated with...,' a metaphor
suggested by the primitive idea that the Deity literally partook
of the sacrifice.

12. appear before me: better as marg. 'see my face.' The
idea that death followed the seeing of God's face, or the desire
to avoid anthropomorphism, caused objection to be taken to
the expression, and the passive form ('appear' = 'be seen') was
substituted.

13 hand, to trample my courts? Bring no more vain obla-
    tions; incense is an abomination unto me; new moon
    and sabbath, the calling of assemblies,—I cannot away
14 with iniquity and the solemn meeting. Your new moons
    and your appointed feasts my soul hateth: they are a
15 trouble unto me; I am weary to bear them. And when
    ye spread forth your hands, I will hide mine eyes from
    you: yea, when ye make many prayers, I will not hear:
16 your hands are full of blood. Wash you, make you
    clean; put away the evil of your doings from before
17 mine eyes; cease to do evil: learn to do well; seek
    judgement, relieve the oppressed, judge the fatherless,
    plead for the widow.

18   Come now, and let us reason together, saith the LORD:
    though your sins be as scarlet, they shall be as white as
    snow; though they be red like crimson, they shall be as
19 wool. If ye be willing and obedient, ye shall eat the
20 good of the land: but if ye refuse and rebel, ye shall be

---

to trample my courts. Follow LXX, and take the words with
v. 13, 'When ye come to see my face, who has required this
(i.e. these many sacrifices) at your hands? Trample my courts
no more...to bring oblations is vain.'

13. iniquity...meeting: i.e. the combination is unendurable.
But rather read, partly following LXX, 'fasting and festal
assembly.'

15. spread...hands: i.e. in the attitude of prayer.

16, 17. The real demand of God:—reformation of character,
righteousness, and justice.

17. relieve the oppressed: marg. 'set right the oppressor.'

18–20. Yahwe's ultimatum.

The free offer of pardon, *v.* 18, seems hard to reconcile with
the context, in which God's favour is clearly stated to depend on
reformation and obedience (16 f., 19 f.). It is perhaps better, in
consideration of Isaiah's argument throughout the passage, to
read 18 *b* interrogatively: 'If your sins be as scarlet, shall they
be white as snow?' The ironical sense preferred by many
recent commentators ('though your sins be..., let them be...')
is less acceptable.

20. ye shall be...sword: a doubtful construction. Read 'ye
shall eat desolation,' a strong antithesis to *v.* 19.

devoured with the sword : for the mouth of the LORD
hath spoken it.

How is the faithful city become an harlot ! she that 21
was full of judgement ! righteousness lodged in her, but
now murderers. Thy silver is become dross, thy wine 22
mixed with water. Thy princes are rebellious, and com- 23
panions of thieves ; every one loveth gifts, and followeth
after rewards : they judge not the fatherless, neither doth
the cause of the widow come unto them.

Therefore saith the Lord, the LORD of hosts, the 24
Mighty One of Israel, Ah, I will ease me of mine adversaries, and avenge me of mine enemies : and I will turn 25
my hand upon thee, and throughly purge away thy dross,
and will take away all thy tin : and I will restore thy 26
judges as at the first, and thy counsellors as at the

21-26. A lament over the degeneracy of Jerusalem, concluding with the threat of judgment and promise of restoration.

The evils complained of are largely social and political, and
reform is to be effected by the restoration of the sound political
conditions of Israel's earlier and better days. In Isaiah's later
prophecies the idea of restoration is less prominent, his gaze
being fixed on the transcendent glory of the future Messianic
kingdom.

The lament is in the *Ḳinah*, or elegiac, rhythm, in which
each line is divided by a caesura into two parts, of which the
first is rather longer than the second, e.g. ' how is she become a
harlot—the faithful city.'

21. harlot. In Hosea i.–iii. this metaphor is made the basis
of a description of Israel's infidelity to Yahwe. Here it is a
mere suggestion, and points rather to general moral deterioration.

24. ease me of : i.e. satisfy my wrath against.

25. throughly : lit. ' as with lye,' alkali used for cleansing
metals, i.e. separating the precious from the baser elements.
But the construction is difficult, and the word for ' lye ' occurs,
in this sense, here only. A plausible emendation is ' in the
furnace.'

tin : rather ' alloy,' the baser element mixed with the precious
metal.

25, 26. Note the parallelism with *vv.* 21–23, the concluding
words of *v.* 26 taking up the first words of *v.* 21, and thus
rounding off the elegy.

beginning : afterward thou shalt be called The city of
27 righteousness, the faithful city. Zion shall be redeemed
with judgement, and her converts with righteousness.
28 But the destruction of the transgressors and the sinners
shall be together, and they that forsake the LORD shall
29 be consumed. For they shall be ashamed of the oaks
which ye have desired, and ye shall be confounded for
30 the gardens that ye have chosen. For ye shall be as
an oak whose leaf fadeth, and as a garden that hath no
31 water. And the strong shall be as tow, and his work as a
spark ; and they shall both burn together, and none shall
quench them.
2   The word that Isaiah the son of Amoz saw concerning
Judah and Jerusalem.

27, 28. A kind of appendix to the poem *vv.* 21-26.

converts : those in Zion who turn to God, and thereby escape
the judgment threatened in *v.* 28.

29-31. The purifying judgment will sweep away superstitious
rites, and expose the folly of worshipping nature, and created
things, rather than the Creator.

29. oaks : marg. 'terebinths,' but really sacred trees of any
species. The 'gardens,' or groves, were the seats of nature
worship, of the cult of sacred trees and wells. The failure of
these deities in the face of the judgment of God suggests the
simile of the decay of the sacred tree, and the drying up of the
sacred well, in *v.* 30.

31. the strong...his work. The imagery is obscure, but if
the translation be correct the idea is that sin, or the sin of
idolatry in particular, itself starts the consuming fire in which
the sinner ('the strong') perishes.

II. Ch. ii.-iv.

This group of oracles, though not necessarily delivered even
approximately at the same time, forms a second distinct section,
belonging in general to an early period in Isaiah's career. There
are suggestions of great material prosperity, accompanied by
moral dissoluteness, by misgovernment on the part of the rulers,
and by something like anarchy in the nation. All this seems to
reflect the condition and fortunes of Judah under Uzziah, Jotham,
and Ahaz.

As at present arranged the group consists of a Messianic

ii. 2–5. *The future glory of Zion.*

And it shall come to pass in the latter days, that the 2
mountain of the LORD'S house shall be established in the
top of the mountains, and shall be exalted above the hills ;
and all nations shall flow unto it.   And many peoples shall 3
go and say, Come ye, and let us go up to the mountain of
the LORD, to the house of the God of Jacob ; and he will

---

prelude (ii. 2–5) ; a series of denunciations and threats of
judgment (ii. 6–iv. 1) ; and a Messianic epilogue (iv. 2–6).

ii. 1.   Editorial superscription to ch. ii.–iv.

word...saw.   The 'word' is the substance of the Divine
revelation through the prophet, who communicates what he has
seen with the eye of spiritual vision.   See on 'vision,' i. 1 ;
and cf. Amos i. 1 ; Micah i. 1.

2–5.   This passage presents a difficult literary problem
owing to its occurrence, in a somewhat fuller form, in Micah iv.
1–5.

Four views find support : (1) That Isaiah is the author, and
that Micah, his younger contemporary, quotes from him.
(2) That Isaiah quotes from Micah. (3) That both prophets
quote a well-known utterance of some earlier prophet. (4) In
view of the fact that the leading ideas of the passage were
certainly current in exilic and post-exilic times, and received
emphasis and confirmation from the circumstances and hopes
of those times, it is urged with much plausibility that the passage
itself is post-exilic and is a late insertion both here and in Micah.

On the whole it may be said that Isaiah is more likely to have
been the author than Micah, and that, while the possibility of
post-exilic insertion must not be ignored, there is no cogent
argument against Isaiah's authorship.

2. in...days.   This general way of indicating the distant
future acquired a special eschatological significance, referring
to the Messianic epoch.   Passages like this mark the transition
from the general to the special use of the phrase.

in the top : marg. reads 'at the head,' thus avoiding the idea
of the physical exaltation of the temple-mountain.   Descriptions
of startling physical changes are sufficiently common in ideal
pictures of the 'latter days,' but it is possible that in this case
the language is purely metaphorical.   The religious pre-eminence
of Zion is what is chiefly emphasized.

teach us of his ways, and we will walk in his paths: for out of Zion shall go forth the law, and the word of the
4 LORD from Jerusalem. And he shall judge between the nations, and shall reprove many peoples: and they shall beat their swords into plowshares, and their spears into pruninghooks: nation shall not lift up sword against nation, neither shall they learn war any more.

5 O house of Jacob, come ye, and let us walk in the light of the LORD.

6-21. The 'Day of Yahwe.'

6 For thou hast forsaken thy people the house of Jacob, because they be filled *with customs* from the east, and *are* soothsayers like the Philistines, and they strike hands
7 with the children of strangers. Their land also is full of silver and gold, neither is there any end of their treasures;

---

3. will teach...will walk: transl. 'that he may teach...and that we may walk.'

law: marg. 'instruction.' See on i. 10.

4. reprove: marg. 'decide concerning.' Yahwe will be acknowledged by all nations as judge or arbitrator, so that wars will be unnecessary. For the idea cf. ix. 5 ff., xi. 6; Hos. ii. 18.

6-21. The humbling of the ungodly pride of Israel, and the destruction of his false gods, in the great 'Day of Yahwe.'

The refrain verses, 10, 11, 17, 19, 21, indicate that this is a poem with a strophic arrangement, though the irregularity of their occurrence points to some dislocation of the text. The 'for' of *v.* 6 suggests that something, possibly the refrain *vv.* 10, 19, has dropped out before it.

6. thou hast forsaken: read with LXX 'he has forsaken.'

because...Philistines: read 'for they are filled with sorcery from the east, and deal in magic like the Philistines.'

strike hands with: i.e. as usually explained, 'form alliances with.' But there may be a reference, not now intelligible, to some form of divination.

7. Isaiah objected on moral and religious grounds, not to the prosperity of the people under Uzziah and Jotham, but to the

their land also is full of horses, neither is there any end of
their chariots. Their land also is full of idols ; they 8
worship the work of their own hands, that which their
own fingers have made. And the mean man is bowed 9
down, and the great man is brought low : therefore forgive them not. Enter into the rock, and hide thee in 10
the dust, from before the terror of the LORD, and from
the glory of his majesty. The lofty looks of man shall 11
be brought low, and the haughtiness of men shall be
bowed down, and the LORD alone shall be exalted in that
day. For there shall be a day of the LORD of hosts 12
upon all that is proud and haughty, and upon all that is
lifted up ; and it shall be brought low : and upon all the 13
cedars of Lebanon, that are high and lifted up, and upon
all the oaks of Bashan ; and upon all the high mountains, 14
and upon all the hills that are lifted up ; and upon every 15
lofty tower, and upon every fenced wall ; and upon all 16

---

luxury, the dependence upon material things, and the foreign
and heathen influences, which this prosperity brought with it.

8. idols: lit. 'nothings' (*ĕlīlīm*), a contemptuous play upon
the word for 'gods' (*ēlīm*).

9. mean man...great man. Two different words for 'man,'
like Lat. *homo* and *vir*. Cf. Ps. xlix. 2, lxii. 9.

The verse may refer to the degradation brought about by
superstitious practices, or, more probably, to the humbling of
men under God's judgment. In either case 'therefore forgive
them not ' is an unsuitable continuation, and is probably corrupt.
The whole verse may be a corruption of the refrain *v.* 11.

10, 11. Two refrain *vv.*, occurring in reverse order, and
with some variations, in *vv.* 17–19. The strophic arrangement
must have suffered disturbance in the transmission of the text.

12. For...upon: marg. 'For Yahwe of hosts hath a day
upon....' The 'Day of Yahwe' means the great interposition
of Yahwe, to which the prophets looked forward, to judge
Israel and the world, and through judgment to purify and
restore. From Amos v. 18 ff. it appears that the Israelites
expected the 'Day of Yahwe' to bring an interposition on their
behalf. The prophets taught that the judgment would fall, not
upon the world on behalf of Israel, but upon Israel and the
world. The judgment is described under the imagery of a
terrific thunderstorm, *vv.* 13–16.

the ships of Tarshish, and upon all pleasant imagery.
17 And the loftiness of man shall be bowed down, and the
haughtiness of men shall be brought low : and the LORD
18 alone shall be exalted in that day.   And the idols shall
19 utterly pass away.   And men shall go into the caves of
the rocks, and into the holes of the earth, from before the
terror of the LORD, and from the glory of his majesty,
20 when he ariseth to shake mightily the earth.   In that day
a man shall cast away his idols of silver, and his idols of
gold, which they made for him to worship, to the moles
21 and to the bats ; to go into the caverns of the rocks, and
into the clefts of the ragged rocks, from before the terror
of the LORD, and from the glory of his majesty, when he
22 ariseth to shake mightily the earth.   Cease ye from man,
whose breath is in his nostrils : for wherein is he to be
accounted of ?

iii. 1-15.   *Social and political dissolution.*

3   For, behold, the Lord, the LORD of hosts, doth take
away from Jerusalem and from Judah stay and staff, the
2 whole stay of bread, and the whole stay of water ; the

---

16.   ships of Tarshish : Phoenician ships trading with
Tartessus in Spain, the farthest limit of early voyages.   The
expression came to be used as a general designation of large
ships, irrespective of their destination.
   pleasant imagery.   The word for 'imagery' occurs only here
and is of quite uncertain meaning.
   17, 18.   See on *vv.* 10, 11 ; *v.* 18, abrupt and fragmentary as
it stands, may be part of the refrain *v.* 17.
   19-21.   These verses consist of a refrain, *v.* 19, repeated in
v. 21, and a prose insertion, *v.* 20, which seems to be a comment
on the destruction of the idols, *v.* 18.
   22.   An obvious interpolation, wanting in LXX.
   whose...nostrils : read 'in whose nostrils is (but) a breath,'
i.e. whose life is but a breath.
   iii. 1.   stay and staff.   The same word in masc. and fem.
form, with the meaning 'every kind of support.'
   the whole...water.   A mistaken gloss, as the 'stay and staff'
are clearly the pillars of the social fabric (*vv.* 2, 3).

mighty man, and the man of war; the judge, and the
prophet, and the diviner, and the ancient; the captain of 3
fifty, and the honourable man, and the counsellor, and the
cunning artificer, and the skilful enchanter. And I will 4
give children to be their princes, and babes shall rule over
them. And the people shall be oppressed, every one by 5
another, and every one by his neighbour: the child shall
behave himself proudly against the ancient, and the base
against the honourable. When a man shall take hold of 6
his brother in the house of his father, *saying*, Thou hast
clothing, be thou our ruler, and let this ruin be under thy
hand: in that day shall he lift up *his voice*, saying, I will 7
not be an healer; for in my house is neither bread nor
clothing: ye shall not make me ruler of the people.
For Jerusalem is ruined, and Judah is fallen: because 8
their tongue and their doings are against the LORD, to
provoke the eyes of his glory. The shew of their 9
countenance doth witness against them; and they declare

---

2. prophet: i.e. professional soothsayer, or member of the
prophetic guild, classed by Isaiah among enchanters and diviners.
Cf. Amos vii. 14 'I am no prophet.'

ancient: marg. 'elder.'

3. honourable: the highly esteemed (cf. Job xxii. 8), or the
favoured (cf. 2 Kings v. 1).

cunning artificer: marg. 'charmer'; lit. 'skilled in (magic)
arts.'

4. babes. This rendering suits the parallel 'children,' but
the noun is abstract, recurring only in lxvi. 4 (E.V. 'delusions').
We may render 'despotic caprice.'

6. a man...his brother: rather 'one man...another.' For
'clothing' read 'cloak.' The idea is that in the general ruin
and confusion any man who has retained his ancestral house,
and has a respectable outer cloak, will be clamorously offered
the position of local judge, or ruler.

7. The man thus chosen will protest that he is no better off
than his neighbours, and that he cannot undertake to bind up
the wounds of the state, and restore the ruin.

9. shew of their countenance: marg. 'their respecting of
persons.' Their flagrant and undisguised partiality in judgment is
a constant witness against them. A less probable rendering is

their sin as Sodom, they hide it not. Woe unto their
10 soul! for they have rewarded evil unto themselves. Say
ye of the righteous, that *it shall be* well *with him* : for
11 they shall eat the fruit of their doings. Woe unto the
wicked ! *it shall be* ill *with him* : for the reward of his
12 hands shall be given him. As for my people, children
are their oppressors, and women rule over them. O my
people, they which lead thee cause thee to err, and destroy
13 the way of thy paths. The LORD standeth up to plead, and
14 standeth to judge the peoples. The LORD will enter into
judgement with the elders of his people, and the princes
thereof : It is ye that have eaten up the vineyard ; the
15 spoil of the poor is in your houses : what mean ye that ye
crush my people, and grind the face of the poor? saith
the Lord, the LORD of hosts.

'the expression of their face,' i.e. sin has stamped itself upon
their faces.

their soul : i.e. themselves: 'Woe to themselves, for they have
done themselves evil.'   The injustice which witnesses against
them will recoil upon themselves.

10, 11. A somewhat weak generalization of the principle
declared in the last clause of *v.* 9; it disturbs the context, and is
probably an interpolation.

Say...righteous : read (with a slight textual change) 'happy
is the righteous,' parallel to ' woe...wicked,' *v.* 11.

12. children...oppressors : transl. ' My people...his ruler
acts like a child, and women govern him.'   The reference is
presumably to the women of the royal harem.

destroy...paths : ' have swallowed up' or ' have confused,'
i.e. effaced, the true ancient path of national dignity and
righteousness.

13-15. A picture of God as judge, vindicating the poor and
down-trodden, and accusing their oppressors.   It forms an impressive conclusion to the preceding denunciation of social
tyranny and anarchy.

14. It is...vineyard. ' Ye' is strongly emphasized. It is ye,
the natural guardians of the vineyard (cf. v. 1-7), who have
yourselves devoured it.

16-24. *A denunciation of the haughty women of Jerusalem.*

Moreover the LORD said, Because the daughters of 16
Zion are haughty, and walk with stretched forth necks and
wanton eyes ; walking and mincing as they go, and
making a tinkling with their feet : therefore the Lord 17
will smite with a scab the crown of the head of the
daughters of Zion, and the LORD will lay bare their secret
parts. In that day the Lord will take away the bravery 18
of their anklets, and the cauls, and the crescents ; the 19
pendants, and the bracelets, and the mufflers ; the head- 20
tires, and the ankle chains, and the sashes, and the
perfume boxes, and the amulets ; the rings, and the nose 21
jewels ; the festival robes, and the mantles, and the 22
shawls, and the satchels ; the hand mirrors, and the fine 23
linen, and the turbans, and the veils. And it shall come 24
to pass, that instead of sweet spices there shall be
rottenness ; and instead of a girdle a rope ; and instead
of well set hair baldness ; and instead of a stomacher a
girding of sackcloth : branding instead of beauty.

---

16. and wanton...feet : transl. ' and ogling with their eyes :
with tripping steps they walk, and with their feet they make
their anklets tinkle.'

18-23. An enumeration of various articles of feminine finery.
As these verses are prose in a poetical context, and as *v.* 24 is
the natural continuation of *v.* 17, there is reason to suspect
interpolation.

18. cauls : a caul is a hair-net ; but render either 'little suns,'
ornaments like the 'crescents'; or ' front-bands,' worn round the
forehead.

20. ankle chains : chains connecting the bangles on the
ankles, and producing the tripping gait and tinkling noise
mentioned in *v.* 16.   Another explanation is ' arm-chain,' a
bracelet worn on the upper arm.

22. satchels : or ' purses,' as in 2 Kings v. 23.

23. hand mirrors : either 'tablets' of polished metal, or
' fine gauze garments.'

24. well set hair : perhaps ' curled locks.'
stomacher : perhaps ' rich garment.'
branding : the symbol of slavery.

iii. 25-iv. 1.   *The desolation of Jerusalem.*

25 Thy men shall fall by the sword, and thy mighty in the
26 war.   And her gates shall lament and mourn ; and she
4 shall be desolate and sit upon the ground.   And seven
women shall take hold of one man in that day, saying,
We will eat our own bread, and wear our own apparel :
only let us be called by thy name ; take thou away
our reproach.

iv. 2-6.   *The redeemed and holy Zion of the
glorious future.*

2   In that day shall the branch of the LORD be beautiful
and glorious, and the fruit of the land shall be excellent
3 and comely for them that are escaped of Israel.   And it
shall come to pass, that he that is left in Zion, and he that
remaineth in Jerusalem, shall be called holy, even every
4 one that is written among the living in Jerusalem : when

25, 26. A personification of Zion, defeated and desolate.
Her gates, usually the resort of a busy crowd, bewail their
desolation, and the city, now become empty, sinks upon the
ground.

iv. 1. The ravages of war have destroyed the male population, and the women can find no man to deliver them from the
shame of childlessness, though promising to earn their own
living, and be no burden upon him.   The women should not be
identified with the haughty ladies of iii. 16-24.

2-6. After the purifying judgment the saved remnant of Judah
will be altogether holy ; the land will be blessed with new and
extraordinary fertility ; and the visible presence of Yahwe will
be a protection against all that is hurtful.

This poem is regarded by many writers as post-exilic, and it is
certainly one that we should more readily attribute to a later
and less skilful hand than Isaiah's.

2. branch...Lord : rather 'growth of Yahwe,' i.e. the growth
due to the special fertility imparted by Yahwe to the soil.   The
expression is parallel to 'fruit of the land.'   The word is used in
Jer. xxiii. 5, xxxiii. 15, of the coming King, the 'shoot of
David,' but the context shows that it should be taken literally
here.   The 'branch' in xi. 1 is not the same word.

3. written...living : those who do not perish in the judgment, and are written in the new burgess-roll, which contains no
unworthy names.

the Lord shall have washed away the filth of the daughters
of Zion, and shall have purged the blood of Jerusalem
from the midst thereof, by the spirit of judgement, and by
the spirit of burning.   And the LORD will create over the 5
whole habitation of mount Zion, and over her assemblies,
a cloud and smoke by day, and the shining of a flaming
fire by night : for over all the glory *shall be spread* a
canopy.   And there shall be a pavilion for a shadow in 6
the day-time from the heat, and for a refuge and for a
covert from storm and from rain.

v. 1-7.   *The vineyard of Yahwe.*

Let me sing for my wellbeloved a song of my beloved **5**
touching his vineyard.   My wellbeloved had a vineyard

---

4.   spirit of burning : rather 'spirit of destruction.'   The
spirit is the Divine energy which is operative not only in the
moral and spiritual sphere (cf. xi. 2, lxi. 1), but also in the
realm of nature (cf. xxxii. 15).
5, 6. Two obscure verses, of which the text is corrupt,
describing, in imagery drawn from the narrative of the Exodus,
the protecting presence of Yahwe. overshadowing Zion with
cloud and flame.

III. Ch. v.

This chapter is isolated and without superscription.   It consists of (*a*) the parable of the Vineyard, *vv.* 1-7 ; (*b*) a series of
'Woes' directed against the private vices and public mal-
administration of the ruling classes, *vv.* 8-24 ; (*c*) a description
of Divine judgment through the instrumentality of Assyrian
invasion, *vv.* 25-30.   The various prophetic addresses in *vv.*
1-24 may be assigned approximately to the same date as
ch. ii.-iv., in the earlier years of Isaiah's public life.   The last
section, *vv.* 25-30, has been misplaced (see on *v.* 25).
v. 1-7. By means of a simple and pointed parable Isaiah
convicts the men of Judah of ingratitude, and proclaims the
approaching punishment.
1.   Read 'I would sing of my Friend, my Friend's song of
his vineyard.'   The text employs two words for 'friend,' but
apparently without distinction in meaning.   The second half of
the line may be translated 'a love-song of his vineyard,' but the
appropriateness of the term is doubtful.

2 in a very fruitful hill: and he made a trench about it, and
gathered out the stones thereof, and planted it with the
choicest vine, and built a tower in the midst of it, and
also hewed out a winepress therein: and he looked that
it should bring forth grapes, and it brought forth wild
3 grapes. And now, O inhabitants of Jerusalem and men of
Judah, judge, I pray you, betwixt me and my vineyard.
4 What could have been done more to my vineyard, that I
have not done in it? wherefore, when I looked that it
should bring forth grapes, brought it forth wild grapes?
5 And now go to; I will tell you what I will do to my vineyard: I will take away the hedge thereof, and it shall be
eaten up; I will break down the fence thereof, and it
6 shall be trodden down: and I will lay it waste; it shall
not be pruned nor hoed; but there shall come up briers
and thorns: I will also command the clouds that they
7 rain no rain upon it. For the vineyard of the LORD of
hosts is the house of Israel, and the men of Judah his
pleasant plant: and he looked for judgement, but behold
oppression; for righteousness, but behold a cry.

---

2. Having obtained a vineyard on a sunny hill-top, a favourable situation, the ' Friend ' dug the soil, cleared it of stones, and
planted choice vines. Then he built a watch-tower, and in
view of the expected vintage, hewed out in the rock a wine-vat
(marg.), into which the grape-juice would flow when the grapes
were trodden in the wine-press. In spite of all his efforts the
grapes were no better than those yielded by wild, untended
vines.
3-6. The owner of the vineyard speaks in the first person,
appealing to the people in order that they may be convicted out
of their own mouths, and finally throwing off all disguise in the
last clause of *v*. 6, where the command of the clouds shows that
Yahwe himself is the speaker.
7. Having allowed his hearers to perceive that his song of
the vineyard was a parable directed against themselves, Isaiah
drives the lesson home, emphasizing it by a pair of ringing
verbal assonances which cannot be reproduced in English.
Yahwe's special care of His people has been wasted; they are
no better than the heathen.

8-24. Denunciations of prevalent vices.

Woe unto them that join house to house, that lay field 8
to field, till there be no room, and ye be made to dwell
alone in the midst of the land! In mine ears *saith* the 9
LORD of hosts, Of a truth many houses shall be desolate,
even great and fair, without inhabitant. For ten acres of 10
vineyard shall yield one bath, and a homer of seed shall
yield *but* an ephah.

Woe unto them that rise up early in the morning, that 11
they may follow strong drink; that tarry late into the
night, till wine inflame them! And the harp and the 12
lute, the tabret and the pipe, and wine, are *in* their feasts:
but they regard not the work of the LORD, neither have
they considered the operation of his hands. Therefore 13
my people are gone into captivity, for lack of knowledge:
and their honourable men are famished, and their
multitude are parched with thirst. Therefore hell hath 14

8-10. A denunciation of the greed of the wealthy, who dis-
possessed the peasant proprietors, so that ownership of land, the
sign and guarantee of independent citizenship, was confined to a
few persons. The threatened punishment is unfruitfulness of the
soil, 10 'yoke' of land ('yoke'=as much as one pair of oxen
could plough in a day) yielding only a 'bath' of wine (about
8 gallons), and seed which should have yielded a 'homer' producing only an 'ephah'=$\frac{1}{10}$ homer, or about 1 bushel.

11-13. A denunciation of the dissipation of the upper classes,
the punishment being exile.

12. but...hands. In the midst of sensuous enjoyments they
ignore Yahwe, and are blind to the impending judgment.

13. for lack of knowledge: rather 'unawares,' showing the
blindness of those who should have been their guides.

famished: read 'exhausted by hunger' (cf. Deut. xxxii. 24),
parallel to 'parched with thirst.'

honourable...multitude: lit. 'glory...tumult,' i.e. the nobility
and the gay throng of pleasure-seekers. The phrases are
parallel, not contrasted.

14. A threat of judgment on the city, probably the conclusion of a denunciation of which the first part has been lost.

enlarged her desire, and opened her mouth without measure : and their glory, and their multitude, and their pomp, and he that rejoiceth among them, descend *into it.*

15 And the mean man is bowed down, and the great man is
16 humbled, and the eyes of the lofty are humbled : but the LORD of hosts is exalted in judgement, and God
17 the Holy One is sanctified in righteousness. Then shall the lambs feed as in their pasture, and the waste places of the fat ones shall wanderers eat.

18   Woe unto them that draw iniquity with cords of vanity,
19 and sin as it were with a cart rope : that say, Let him make speed, let him hasten his work, that we may see it : and let the counsel of the Holy One of Israel draw nigh and come, that we may know it !

20   Woe unto them that call evil good, and good evil; that put darkness for light, and light for darkness ; that put bitter for sweet, and sweet for bitter!

21   Woe unto them that are wise in their own eyes, and prudent in their own sight !

22   Woe unto them that are mighty to drink wine, and men

---

hell : better 'Sheol,' or 'Hades,' the dark, inevitable, insatiable underworld. See on xiv. 9.

and their...into it : transl. 'and down goes her pomp, her tumult, and her uproar (the noise of revelry), and all that is jubilant in her.' Note the feminine possessives, showing that the reference is now to the city.

15, 16. An interpolated reminiscence of ii. 9, 11, 17.

17. This verse concludes the description of desolation begun in *v.* 14. Lambs will graze among the ruins of the fallen city.

wanderers : read 'kids,' parallel to 'lambs.'

18, 19. A denunciation of scornful scepticism. Those who, in wilful and hardened folly, made sport of the Divine judgment were dragging sin and its inevitable punishment upon themselves.

20-23. Three short and probably fragmentary denunciations (1) of sophistical perversions of recognized moral standards, *v.* 20 ; (2) of blind self-conceit, *v.* 21 ; (3) of the dissolute lives and corrupt practices of the judges, *vv.* 22, 23.

22. mighty...strong drink. The heroes of the bottle were skilled in compounding potent cups. Cf. Prov. xxiii. 30.

of strength to mingle strong drink: which justify the 23
wicked for a reward, and take away the righteousness of
the righteous from him! Therefore as the tongue of fire 24
devoureth the stubble, and as the dry grass sinketh down
in the flame, so their root shall be as rottenness, and
their blossom shall go up as dust: because they have
rejected the law of the LORD of hosts, and despised the
word of the Holy One of Israel.

25-30. *The last phase of the Divine judgment.*

Therefore is the anger of the LORD kindled against his 25
people, and he hath stretched forth his hand against them,
and hath smitten them, and the hills did tremble, and
their carcases were as refuse in the midst of the streets.
For all this his anger is not turned away, but his hand is
stretched out still. And he will lift up an ensign to the 26
nations from far, and will hiss for them from the end of

---

23. take away...him: i.e. declare him guilty.
24. A final threat of punishment, not strictly applicable to
any of the immediately preceding denunciations, but suitable
as the conclusion of the whole passage, and laying stress on the
fundamental sin of rejecting the Divine message delivered by the
prophet.

law...word: see on i. 10.
25-30. These verses were originally the conclusion, not of *vv.*
8-24, but of the series of judgments ix. 8-x. 4. Note (1) the refrain
at the end of *v.* 25 and cf. ix. 12, 17, 21, and x. 4. (2) The
word 'therefore' is not the same as in *vv.* 13, 14, 24, but agrees
with ix. 17. (3) *v.* 24 is the appropriate conclusion of *vv.* 8-24,
whereas x. 4 leaves the hand still stretched out: *vv.* 25-30
supply the climax—the desolation is complete, and Yahwe's
hand is stretched out no more.

As *v.* 25 is too short to be an entire strophe it is probable
that some lines were lost when the passage was misplaced. The
object of denunciation is not Judah, but North Israel. See on
ix. 8-x. 4.
26. nations: read 'nation.' The invaders are not named,
but are clearly the Assyrians. Note the emphasis on archers,
cavalry, and chariots, all characteristic of the Assyrians.

hiss: as a bee-keeper calls the swarm together. Cf. vii. 18.

the earth: and, behold, they shall come with speed
27 swiftly: none shall be weary nor stumble among them;
none shall slumber nor sleep; neither shall the girdle of
their loins be loosed, nor the latchet of their shoes be
28 broken: whose arrows are sharp, and all their bows bent;
their horses' hoofs shall be counted like flint, and their
29 wheels like a whirlwind: their roaring shall be like a lion,
they shall roar like young lions: yea, they shall roar, and
lay hold of the prey, and carry it away safe, and there
30 shall be none to deliver. And they shall roar against
them in that day like the roaring of the sea: and if one
look unto the land, behold darkness *and* distress, and the
light is darkened in the clouds thereof.

vi. *The Divine call to the prophetic ministry.*

6   In the year that king Uzziah died I saw the Lord
sitting upon a throne, high and lifted up, and his train

---

28. shall be...flint: i.e. are to be imagined as being like
flint.   The cavalry will be able to surmount the difficulties even
of a rocky country like Palestine.

29. The Assyrian battle-cry is like the roar of a lion leaping
on his prey, portending immediate and complete destruction.

30. An obscure verse of uncertain text and doubtful authenticity.   The last words of *v.* 29 suitably conclude the vivid
portrayal of irretrievable disaster.

IV. Ch. vi.–ix. 7.

A series of incidents and prophecies belonging to the early
years of Isaiah's public career, more especially to the time of the
Syro-Ephraimitic war.

In ch. vi Isaiah describes, in language of splendid simplicity, the
great experience which inaugurated his prophetic work.   The language is figurative in the sense that what was visible to the eye,
and audible to the ear, of the spirit, is described as having been
actually seen and heard.   But Isaiah records a real experience,
occurring in the place and at the time stated.   In the year of
Uzziah's death (c. 740 B.C.), in the temple, and possibly amid a
crowd of worshippers, Isaiah saw Yahwe exalted in majesty
and holiness, and received from Him his commission as a
preacher of righteousness and of judgment.   Filled with an overwhelming sense of the Divine presence, the prophet saw with

filled the temple. Above him stood the seraphim : each 2
one had six wings ; with twain he covered his face, and
with twain he covered his feet, and with twain he did fly.
And one cried unto another, and said, Holy, holy, holy, 3

---

terrible clearness the contrast of the Divine holiness and his own
and the people's uncleanness ; he experienced the cleansing power
of complete submission to the Divine will ; and he went forth to
deliver the Divine message as he had received it, even though
the effect of its proclamation would be to make the sins of the
people blacker and their hearts harder.

The statement of the date indicates that some years elapsed
before the description of the vision was written. In the interval
Isaiah had learned by experience what the effect of his message
was, and that experience would intensify the impression made
upon him by the circumstances of his call to the prophetic
ministry. But we need not suppose that his subsequent ex-
periences coloured his description of his inaugural vision.

vi. 1. his...temple. Yahwe appeared in the vision in human
form, but Isaiah did not see His face. The skirts of His
garments filled the entire temple, draping the Divine Majesty
even from the spiritual gaze of the prophet.

2. seraphim : Yahwe's attendant ministers, who 'stood
over' Him, in readiness to execute His commands. These
beings, described here in symbolic language, are mentioned
nowhere else in Scripture, though their solemn chant is echoed
by the four 'living creatures' of Rev. iv. 8. The origin of the
conception is obscure. The word is used of the fiery serpents
which tormented the Israelites in the wilderness (Num. xxi. 6 ;
Deut. viii. 15), and also of a 'fiery flying serpent,' ch. xiv. 29,
xxx. 6. A brazen serpent formed part of the furniture of the
temple, in commemoration of the incident in the wilderness,
and this may have suggested the conception of fiery beings in
attendance on Yahwe, winged like the flying *saraph* of ch. xiv.
29 and xxx. 6, but in form more human than serpentine. The
nearest parallels in ancient mythology are those of the Egyptian
seref, a winged griffin represented as guarding tombs, and the
flying dragons of Arabia. More important is the analogy of the
Cherubim, which were also winged ministers of Yahwe. This
analogy probably accounts for the form in which the flying
saraph of popular mythology—perhaps representing the serpent-
like lightning, as the Cherub represented the thunder-cloud—
appears in Isaiah's vision.

3. The thrice-repeated 'Holy' expresses the supreme
attribute of God, His essential nature. The original meaning
of holiness in O.T. was separation from all that is common and

is the LORD of hosts : the whole earth is full of his glory.
4 And the foundations of the thresholds were moved at the
voice of him that cried, and the house was filled with
5 smoke. Then said I, Woe is me! for I am undone ;
because I am a man of unclean lips, and I dwell in the
midst of a people of unclean lips : for mine eyes have
6 seen the King, the LORD of hosts. Then flew one of the
seraphim unto me, having a live coal in his hand, which
7 he had taken with the tongs from off the altar : and he
touched my mouth with it, and said, Lo, this hath touched
thy lips ; and thine iniquity is taken away, and thy sin
8 purged. And I heard the voice of the Lord, saying,
Whom shall I send, and who will go for us? Then I said,
9 Here am I ; send me. And he said, Go, and tell this

---

unclean. As an attribute of God it expresses His exaltation
above the world and all natural forces, and His complete
freedom from all that makes men imperfect and impure. In
the case of persons or things dedicated to the service of God, the
ceremonial idea of holiness predominated over the ethical, and
the holiness of God was strictly His awful and solitary grandeur
rather than His moral perfection. But to the prophets moral
righteousness was an integral feature of the Divine holiness,
and this ethical character of God is the keynote of their
preaching. Hence Isaiah's first emotion when the sense of the
Divine holiness swept over him was a prostrating consciousness
of sin.

4. The smoke symbolizes the Divine abhorrence of sin.

5. Under a crushing sense of moral impurity Isaiah cries out
that he and the whole people were unfit to worship the infinitely
holy God.

6, 7. The touching of the lips with a hot stone from the
altar was a symbol of cleansing by contact with the Divine
holiness. The unclean lips are fitted for worship and service by
the scorching flame that consumes all that is opposed to the
Divine will, but purifies without destroying the submissive soul,
conscious of its need.

8. Deliverance from the crushing sense of sin and impurity is
followed immediately by the call to service. The eager response
comes from lips still hot from the purifying fire.

9-12. Isaiah's commission was to preach to a generation
morally incapable of understanding his message and fulfilling
the demands of God. The fire of the Divine holiness which

people, Hear ye indeed, but understand not ; and see ye
indeed, but perceive not. Make the heart of this people 10
fat, and make their ears heavy, and shut their eyes ; lest
they see with their eyes, and hear with their ears, and
understand with their heart, and turn again, and be healed.
Then said I, Lord, how long? And he answered, Until 11
cities be waste without inhabitant, and houses without
man, and the land become utterly waste, and the LORD 12
have removed men far away, and the forsaken places be
many in the midst of the land. And if there be yet a 13
tenth in it, it shall again be eaten up : as a terebinth, and
as an oak, whose stock remaineth, when they are felled ;
so the holy seed is the stock thereof.

---

had cleansed him must destroy them. The more they were
taught of the Divine will the more violent would be their re-
action against it, and the deeper would be their guilt. They
were incurable, and Isaiah's prophetic work could only intensify
their hardened blindness, and hasten the catastrophe. To the
cry ' How long?' the answer is that the judgment on that
generation is final, and will be consummated in the utter desolation of the land.

13. An obscure verse. The first clause is naturally interpreted as meaning that should a tenth of the people survive
the great catastrophe, a further judgment will utterly destroy
them. The second clause appears to speak of a stump escaping
destruction when a tree is felled ; but in view of the preceding
clause this should mean that after the felling of the tree a further
effort is necessary to destroy the stump. The third clause, which
is omitted in LXX, and is therefore of doubtful authenticity,
contradicts this interpretation, and encourages the people to hope
that a remnant will be saved to form the seed of a new and
happier generation. As the text stands it must be taken as
a threat of total destruction, even of the last tenth ; and the
closing words must be regarded as a consolatory gloss. On
the other hand the idea that a remnant would be saved is a
characteristic element of Isaiah's preaching, symbolized in the
name Shear-jashub (vii. 3), and the possibility of a reference to
it in this verse cannot be absolutely excluded.

vii. 1–17. *Isaiah's interview with Ahaz, and the prophecy of the birth of Immanuel.*

7 And it came to pass in the days of Ahaz the son of Jotham, the son of Uzziah, king of Judah, that Rezin the king of Syria, and Pekah the son of Remaliah, king of Israel, went up to Jerusalem to war against it; but **2** could not prevail against it. And it was told the house of David, saying, Syria is confederate with Ephraim. And his heart was moved, and the heart of his people, as the trees of the forest are moved with the wind.

3 Then said the LORD unto Isaiah, Go forth now to meet Ahaz, thou, and Shear-jashub thy son, at the end of the

vii. 1–17. The occasion of this prophecy was the Syro-Ephraim-itish campaign against Judah, c. 735 B.C. Syria and Ephraim had combined against Judah, with the object of dethroning the dynasty, and destroying the real independence of the people. So at least Ahaz and his advisers believed. The alliance had the effect of frightening the weak and incompetent king, who proceeded to seek deliverance by calling in the aid' of Assyria against the allies. Against this unnecessary and highly danger-ous step Isaiah interposed a vehement remonstrance alike on political and religious grounds. In order to be delivered from an insignificant peril Ahaz was courting certain subjugation. Further, his action implied want of faith in Yahwe, and, in Isaiah's eyes, amounted almost to apostasy.

1. An editorial insertion supplying later readers with the genealogy of Ahaz, and a summary description of the whole situation, based on 2 Kings xvi. 5.

prevail: rather 'fight,' i.e. proceed from blockade to actual assault.

2. Syria…Ephraim. 'Syria has settled in Ephraim' like a swarm of bees; cf. *v.* 19, where the same word is translated 'rest.' Exaggerated reports of the size of the Syrian army were brought to the 'house of David,' i.e. the royal family, which felt itself to be threatened with extinction.

3. Shear-jashub: 'a remnant shall turn,' i.e. turn from sin to God. The name symbolizes at once the threat of judgment and Isaiah's hope that even in the generation whose doom he was compelled to announce there would be found the nucleus of a God-fearing people.

conduit of the upper pool, in the high way of the fuller's
field ; and say unto him, Take heed, and be quiet ; fear 4
not, neither let thine heart be faint, because of these two
tails of smoking firebrands, for the fierce anger of Rezin
and Syria, and of the son of Remaliah. Because Syria 5
hath counselled evil against thee, Ephraim *also*, and the
son of Remaliah, saying, Let us go up against Judah, and 6
vex it, and let us make a breach therein for us, and set up
a king in the midst of it, even the son of Tabeel : thus 7
saith the Lord GOD, It shall not stand, neither shall it
come to pass. For the head of Syria is Damascus, and 8
the head of Damascus is Rezin : and within threescore
and five years shall Ephraim be broken in pieces, that it
be not a people : and the head of Ephraim is Samaria, 9

---

conduit...field : cf. xxxvi. 2. The pool has been con-
jecturally identified (1) with the Mamilla pool on the west of
the city, (2) with a recently discovered reservoir near the pool of
Siloam on the south-east, (3) with a supposed pool feeding a
conduit which passes into the city near the Damascus gate on
the north. The evidence is inconclusive. In the event of a
siege the water supply was of first importance, and Ahaz was
presumably inspecting its defences.

4. son of Remaliah : a contemptuous reference to Pekah's
humble origin.

6. son of Tabeel : another obscure person, probably a
Syrian, who was to be set up as puppet-king of Judah, which
would thus become practically subject to Syria. It may reasonably be conjectured that Syria's object was to control Judah's
policy in view of Assyrian aggression. Ahaz's counter-move
was to throw himself into the arms of Assyria.

8, 9. Rezin and Pekah are merely human rulers without
power or importance outside their own borders, whereas Judah
may trust in a Divine ruler. For Ahaz faith—in the first instance
acceptance of the word of the prophet speaking in the name of
God—is the great condition of security. This is perhaps (but see
Gen. xv. 6) the first clear statement in O.T. of the fundamental
value and importance of faith, by which is meant confidence in
God's care and guidance, and obedience to His declared will.

v. 8 *b*, **and within...people**, interrupts the context, and is to
be regarded as a gloss to *v.* 9 *a*. What precise event is referred
to is uncertain. The date indicated is c. 670–668 B.C., and it is
possible that the reference is to the settlement of Gentile colonists

and the head of Samaria is Remaliah's son. If ye will
not believe, surely ye shall not be established.

10
11   And the LORD spake again unto Ahaz, saying, Ask thee
a sign of the LORD thy God ; ask it either in the depth,
12 or in the height above. But Ahaz said, I will not ask,
13 neither will I tempt the LORD. And he said, Hear ye
now, O house of David ; is it a small thing for you to weary
14 men, that ye will weary my God also? Therefore the
Lord himself shall give you a sign ; behold, a virgin shall
conceive, and bear a son, and shall call his name
15 Immanuel. Butter and honey shall he eat, when he

---

in Samaria by Esar-haddon (Ezra iv. 2) and Assurbanipal
(Asnappar, Ezra iv. 10), as the death of the former and the
accession of the latter took place in 669/8 B.C.

11. ask it...above : read ' going deep down to Sheol, or
high up to the height.' Ahaz is offered the widest possible
range of choice.

12. tempt : ' put to the test.' Ahaz did not doubt that the
sign would be given. What he lacked was the faith that trusts
and obeys.

13. to weary men. Isaiah is doubtless thinking of rebuffs
which he himself had suffered at the hands of the king and his
immediate circle.

14. himself. The pronoun is emphatic. Ahaz had declined
to choose a sign : he must now accept one of God's choosing.

virgin : rather ' young woman.' The word does not connote
virginity, and had the miracle of a virgin-birth been part of the
sign, Isaiah would certainly have used the regular word for
' virgin,' and so have made his meaning clear. Who the young
mother was is not in any way indicated, and it is therefore
reasonable to suppose that her personality was not of importance to the sign.

Immanuel : ' with us God.' The name symbolizes in the first
instance God's presence and help in the deliverance of the
land from the Syrian and Ephraimitish invaders. The name
alone, given by the mother in a moment of national rejoicing,
as the name Ichabod was given in the hour 'of national
disaster (1 Sam. iv. 21), may have been the important element in the sign, and in that case it would not be necessary to
suppose that any particular child is meant. But this interpretation does not account for the dignity and solemnity of the
prediction, and it is more probable that the prophet had in mind
the personality and history of a particular child bearing this

knoweth to refuse the evil, and choose the good. For 16
before the child shall know to refuse the evil, and choose
the good, the land whose two kings thou abhorrest shall
be forsaken. The LORD shall bring upon thee, and upon 17
thy people, and upon thy father's house, days that have
not come, from the day that Ephraim departed from
Judah ; *even* the king of Assyria.

---

symbolic name. No indication, however, is given, which might
lead to the identification of the child.

15. Butter, or rather, sour milk, and wild honey form the
rough fare of the desert or of a desolate country (cf. *v.* 22).

when...good : i.e. when he has passed out of infancy, and is
able to discriminate the pleasant and the painful, the good and
the hurtful, in a physical sense.

The verse is thus a prediction of the desolation of Judah
shortly after its deliverance from the Syro-Ephraimitish invasion.
Its position is somewhat awkward, and its genuineness is doubted
by many critics. In any case, however, the desolation of Judah
is emphatically predicted in *vv.* 17 and 18–25.

16. The desolation of Syria and Ephraim will take place
while Immanuel is still an infant.

17. The result of the unbelief of Ahaz and his foolish policy
will be a disaster comparable only to the loss to the Davidic
dynasty of the ten tribes in the reign of Rehoboam. Of this
disaster Immanuel was the sign.

The sign of Immanuel. The object of the sign originally
offered was to convince Ahaz that God would deliver him from
the danger which he feared. The sign actually given had the
same object, but with the vital difference that its occurrence,
accompanied by the deliverance of which it was the symbol,
would remind the king of his own unbelief, and of the consequence
of unbelief threatened in *v.* 9. The deliverance was itself part
of the sign, which, essentially modified by the refusal of Ahaz
in *v.* 12, and prefaced by the prophet's indignant outburst in
v. 13, had assumed a sinister aspect, and was a sign of doom.
The name ' Immanuel ' may have been a name of hope for the
' Remnant ' which was to be the seed of a holy people, but for
Ahaz and the whole generation which shared his unbelief the sign
was pregnant with wrath and judgment. This remains true even
if we follow the critics who omit *v.* 15, and limit the *immediate*
significance of the sign of Immanuel to Judah's deliverance and
the desolation of Syria and Ephraim promised in *v.* 16. It may
be that the purport of the sign does not go further than this
immediate deliverance, and the subsequent judgment. On the

18-25. Predictions of invasion and desolation.

18 And it shall come to pass in that day, that the LORD
shall hiss for the fly that is in the uttermost part of the
rivers of Egypt, and for the bee that is in the land of
19 Assyria. And they shall come, and shall rest all of them
in the desolate valleys, and in the holes of the rocks, and
upon all thorns, and upon all pastures.

20 In that day shall the Lord shave with a razor that is
hired, *which is* in the parts beyond the River, *even* with
the king of Assyria, the head and the hair of the feet:
and it shall also consume the beard.

---

other hand Isaiah certainly believed that the judgment would be
followed by the restoration to peace and prosperity of a regenerate and God-fearing people, and in the following chapter
(see viii. 8, 10) the name Immanuel is the watchword of this
hope. It is therefore not unreasonable to suppose that Isaiah
saw in the child whose birth he predicts in such a striking and
almost mysterious manner the embodiment of his hope, and the
actual leader of the Remnant, a witness at his birth to the coming
judgment, and throughout his life to the presence of God with
those who waited in faith for the restoration that would succeed
the judgment. If this be so the passage is the first expression
of the idea of a personal Messiah, and may properly be compared with ix. 2–7 and xi. 1–9. In this Messianic sense it is
quoted in Matt. i. 22, 23. It is true that events did not move as
rapidly as Isaiah anticipated, and that the child whose name was
a sign to Ahaz did not prove to be the Messiah. But this want
of perspective and of detailed fulfilment is characteristic of
Messianic prophecy, and does not prove that Isaiah did not
attach Messianic conceptions to the person of Immanuel.

18–25. A series of short predictions of invasion and
desolation, compiled from Isaiah's prophecies without any
precise indication of date.

18. Judah lay between Egypt and Assyria, and was thus
exposed on both sides to the aggression of the rival empires.
The similes of the fly and the bee are appropriate to the two
countries.

19. desolate valleys : rather ' precipitous defiles.'

20. hired : i.e. by God, but possibly with an allusion to the
policy of Ahaz in hiring the help of Assyria by paying tribute
(2 Kings xvi. 7–18).

And it shall come to pass in that day, that a man shall 21
nourish a young cow, and two sheep ; and it shall come 22
to pass, for the abundance of milk that they shall give he
shall eat butter : for butter and honey shall every one eat
that is left in the midst of the land.

And it shall come to pass in that day, that every place, 23
where there were a thousand vines at a thousand silver-
lings, shall even be for briers and thorns. With arrows 24
and with bow shall one come thither ; because all the land
shall be briers and thorns. And all the hills that were 25
digged with the mattock, thou shalt not come thither for
fear of briers and thorns, but it shall be for the sending
forth of oxen, and for the treading of sheep.

viii. 1–18.   *Oracles from the period of the Syro-Ephraimitic war.*

1–4.   *The conquest of Damascus and Samaria.*

And the LORD said unto me, Take thee a great tablet, **8**
and write upon it with the pen of a man, For Maher-
shalal-hash-baz ; and I will take unto me faithful witnesses 2
to record, Uriah the priest, and Zechariah the son of
Jeberechiah. And I went unto the prophetess ; and she 3
conceived, and bare a son. Then said the LORD unto

21, 22. The desolation of the land will reduce the inhabitants
to the occupation and the fare of shepherds (cf. *v.* 15).

23–25. Agriculture will cease, good vineyards will be overrun
with briers, and the whole land will be a waste, occupied only
by shepherds and hunters.

viii. 1. with...man : marg. ' in common characters,' that all
might read and understand.

Maher-shalal-hash-baz : ' speed-spoil-hurry-booty ' : either
' spoil speeds, booty hurries,' or a description of the king of
Assyria, ' speeding to the spoil, hurrying to the prey.'

2. and I...me : read ' and take for me ' (LXX).

faithful witnesses : persons of repute, whose evidence would
be accepted by the people. Uriah is mentioned in 2 Kings xvi.
10–16 ; Zechariah is otherwise unknown.

3. prophetess. The title does not imply that Isaiah's wife
herself exercised any prophetic function.

4 me, Call his name Maher-shalal-hash-baz. For before
the child shall have knowledge to cry, My father, and, My
mother, the riches of Damascus and the spoil of Samaria
shall be carried away before the king of Assyria.

5-8. *The doom of Judah.*

5 And the LORD spake unto me yet again, saying, For-
6 asmuch as this people hath refused the waters of Shiloah
that go softly, and rejoice in Rezin and Remaliah's son ;
7 now therefore, behold, the Lord bringeth up upon them
the waters of the River, strong and many, *even* the king of
Assyria and all his glory : and he shall come up over all his
channels, and go over all his banks : and he shall sweep
8 onward into Judah ; he shall overflow and pass through ; he
shall reach even to the neck ; and the stretching out of
his wings shall fill the breadth of thy land, O Immanuel.

----

4. The final movement of Assyria against Syria and Israel
began in 734 B.C. Damascus fell in 732 and Samaria in 722/1.
Vv. 1-4 may be dated 735, within a year of the beginning of the
end.

6. waters...softly. The metaphor of the gentle and easy flow
of water along an aqueduct describes the noiseless and beneficent
presence in Zion of Yahwe, Whom Ahaz refused to trust.
The well-known tunnel connecting St Mary's spring with the
pool of Siloam is ascribed to the reign of Hezekiah, and some
earlier aqueduct may have suggested the image.

rejoice in : read ' faint before,' the result and the sign of
their want of faith.

7. the River : the Euphrates, a symbol of the Assyrian
power.

8. he shall overflow...through: rather 'flooding and overflowing.'

stretching...wings. The metaphor of the overflowing Euphrates gives place to that of a bird of prey hovering over the
land.

thy...Immanuel : read ' the land, for with us is God,' as in
v. 10. The expression is Isaiah's watchword in predicting both
the doom of the faithless people and the ultimate deliverance of
the Remnant.

9, 10. A triumphant challenge to the heathen nations.

Make an uproar, O ye peoples, and ye shall be 9
broken in pieces; and give ear, all ye of far countries :
gird yourselves, and ye shall be broken in pieces ; gird
yourselves, and ye shall be broken in pieces. Take coun- 10
sel together, and it shall be brought to nought; speak
the word, and it shall not stand : for God is with us.

11-15. Yahwe the true object of fear.

For the LORD spake thus to me with a strong hand, and 11
instructed me that I should not walk in the way of this
people, saying, Say ye not, A conspiracy, concerning all 12
whereof this people shall say, A conspiracy ; neither fear
ye their fear, nor be in dread *thereof*. The LORD of hosts, 13
him shall ye sanctify; and let him be your fear, and let him
be your dread. And he shall be for a sanctuary ; but for a 14
stone of stumbling and for a rock of offence to both the
houses of Israel, for a gin and for a snare to the inhabitants
of Jerusalem. And many shall stumble thereon, and fall, 15
and be broken, and be snared, and be taken.

9, 10. The heathen nations, irresistible when executing the
Divine purpose of chastisement, will be powerless when Yahwe
intervenes to succour His faithful ones.

9. Make an uproar: transl. 'be enraged': or, possibly, read
with LXX 'know,' parallel to 'give ear.'

and...pieces : transl. 'and be dismayed.'

10. speak the word : i.e. proclaim your purpose.

11. with...me : transl. 'while His hand held me fast, to
warn me.'

12. conspiracy : the coalition of Rezin and Pekah, which
had thrown the king and the people into such unnecessary
agitation.

13. sanctify : 'count holy,' regard as the object of trust and
obedience.

14. sanctuary: i.e. for protection, an asylum; cf. Ez. xi. 16.
To the faithful Yahwe is a refuge and protection ; to the mass of
the people, who fall because they cannot fulfil His moral and
spiritual demands, He is a stone of stumbling.

15. thereon: on the stone and snare. The A.V. rendering
'many among them' is also possible.

*16–18.   Isaiah abandons his public ministry for a time, and
devotes himself to the instruction of his disciples.*

16   Bind thou up the testimony, seal the law among my
17 disciples.   And I will wait for the LORD, that hideth his
face from the house of Jacob, and I will look for him.
18 Behold, I and the children whom the LORD hath given
me are for signs and for wonders in Israel from the LORD
of hosts, which dwelleth in mount Zion.

viii. 19–ix. 7.   *Darkness and dawn.*

19–22.   *Gross darkness.*

19   And when they shall say unto you, Seek unto them
that have familiar spirits and unto the wizards, that chirp
and that mutter : should not a people seek unto their
God ? on behalf of the living *should they seek* unto the
20 dead?   To the law and to the testimony ! if they speak

---

16. Bind thou up...seal. The command is addressed by God
to the prophet ; but the absence of any introductory words is
striking, and the change of person in *v.* 17 is abrupt.   Some
prefer to take the verbs as infinitive absolute, in the sense ' I
must bind...seal.'

law : rather ' instruction.'   See on i. 10.

18. I...children. Isaiah's own name ('salvation of Yahwe '),
and his entire ministry of warning and exhortation, as well as
the significant names given to his sons, Shear-jashub and Maher-
shalal-hash-baz, were signs and portents alike of doom and
restoration.

19-22. The text of these obscure verses is corrupt, and the
translation uncertain.

19. Seek...wizards : 'ask of the spirits and of the necro-
mancers.'

should...dead : possibly the answer to be given to the suggestion of necromancy—' ask not of the dead, but of God '; but
more naturally taken as an argument in support of the superstitious practice—' whom can we consult but God and the
dead ?' necromancy being superstitiously regarded as a means of
revelation.

20. The sense depends on the rendering of *v.* 19.   If
' should...dead ' be the answer to 19 *a*, then ' to the instruction
and the testimony ' is the cry of the foolish people when it is too
late—' surely they will speak according to this word when there

not according to this word, surely there is no morning for
them.   And they shall pass through it, hardly bestead and 21
hungry : and it shall come to pass that, when they shall
be hungry, they shall fret themselves, and curse by their
king and by their God, and turn their faces upward : and 22
they shall look unto the earth, and behold, distress and
darkness, the gloom of anguish ; and into thick darkness
they shall be driven away.   But there shall be no gloom 9
to her that was in anguish.   In the former time he
brought into contempt the land of Zebulun and the land
of Naphtali, but in the latter time hath he made it glorious,
by the way of the sea, beyond Jordan, Galilee of the nations.

---

is no dawn for them,' only when their darkness has become
hopeless.   But taking both clauses of *v.* 19 as the words of the
superstitious people we find the answer to them in 'to the
instruction and the testimony !'—where the true revelation is to
be found ; and read further 'surely they speak according to
this word (i.e. as in *v.* 19) for whom there is no dawn.'

21, 22.   Read 'and he (either the whole people or an
individual) passes through it (i.e. the land, a clause containing
the antecedent of the pronoun having dropped out), faint and
famished, and when he is famished he breaks out in anger, and
curses his king and his God, and looks upward, and looks to the
ground, and behold, distress and darkness, painful gloom, and
into darkness is he driven.'   The last clause may be ' but the
darkness will be driven away,' a gloss leading up to the following
verse.

ix. 1.   But...anguish : lit. ' But (or 'for,' according to the
interpretation of the end of viii. 22) [there is] no gloom to her
(i.e. the land) to whom [is] distress.'   R.V. supplies first a
future tense and then a past, and no better rendering of this
unintelligible sentence has been suggested.   The whole verse is
a transition from the darkness of viii. 19–22 to the Messianic
light of *vv.* 2–7.

way of the sea : possibly the road from Acre to Damascus,
the Via Maris of the Crusaders.   There is nothing to determine
whether the reference is to the Mediterranean or to the Sea
of Galilee.

Galilee : rather 'circuit,' the district on the northern border
of Palestine, with a mixed population.   These northern regions
are specially mentioned because they were the first to experience
the desolating judgment.

ix. 2-7. *The Messianic dawn and glory.*

2 The people that walked in darkness have seen a great
 light : they that dwelt in the land of the shadow of
3 death, upon them hath the light shined. Thou hast
 multiplied the nation, thou hast increased their joy : they
 joy before thee according to the joy in harvest, as men
4 rejoice when they divide the spoil. For the yoke of his
 burden, and the staff of his shoulder, the rod of his
 oppressor, thou hast broken as in the day of Midian.
5 For all the armour of the armed man in the tumult, and
 the garments rolled in blood, shall even be for burning,
6 for fuel of fire. For unto us a child is born, unto us a
 son is given ; and the government shall be upon his
 shoulder : and his name shall be called Wonderful,
 Counsellor, Mighty God, Everlasting Father, Prince of

2—7. The authenticity of this poem is denied by many critics,
but their arguments are not conclusive. It may owe its present
position to an editor's desire to provide a contrast to the preceding picture of gloom and desolation, but its real affinity is
with x. 5–xi. 9, and it should possibly be dated shortly before
the deliverance of Jerusalem in 701 B.C. Cf. *v.* 4 with x. 26, 27,
and the whole passage with xi. 1–9.

3. **nation** : read, with slight change of text, 'exultation.'

4. **For.** Three causes of exultation are given : deliverance,
v. 4 ; peace, *v.* 5 ; the birth and reign of the Messiah, *vv.* 6, 7.

staff...shoulder: i.e. the staff with which his (Israel's) back
is beaten.

day of Midian : the day (of battle) on which the Midianites
were overwhelmingly defeated, and Israel was delivered from
their domination (Jud. vi.–viii.).

5. Transl. 'For every boot of him that is heavily booted, and
every cloak rolled in blood, shall be....' The word translated
'in the tumult' refers to the noisy tread of the heavy military
boot.

6. The birth of the Messianic king synchronizes roughly with
the completion of the deliverance.

Wonderful...Peace : rather 'Wonder-Counsellor, Hero-God,
the ever Fatherly, Prince of Peace.' The wisdom and might of
God are exhibited in the character and achievements of the
Prince born to the restored people. The third title means that
the king's fatherly care of his people is unceasing.

Peace. Of the increase of his government and of peace 7
there shall be no end, upon the throne of David, and
upon his kingdom, to establish it, and to uphold it with
judgement and with righteousness from henceforth even
for ever. The zeal of the LORD of hosts shall perform
this.

*ix. 8–x. 4. Yahwe's hand stretched out in wrath. The stages
of the Divine judgment on North Israel.*

8–12. Judgment at the hands of foreign enemies.

The Lord sent a word into Jacob, and it hath lighted 8
upon Israel. And all the people shall know, *even* Ephraim 9
and the inhabitant of Samaria, that say in pride and in
stoutness of heart, The bricks are fallen, but we will 10

---

7. Of...end: read 'Great is his rule, and it makes for
endless peace.'
zeal...Lord: Yahwe's jealous maintenance of His own honour
and of the people by whom He is honoured.

V. Ch. ix. 8–x. 4 (+ v. 25–30).

The poem is divided into four strophes, each closing with the
refrain ix. 12, 17, 21, x. 4. It is probable that the close of a
fifth strophe is preserved in v. 25, and that v. 26–30 formed the
original conclusion of the whole poem (see on v. 25–30). The
entire oracle is directed against North Israel. The date is
between 740 and 735, before the Syro-Ephraimitish alliance,
of which there is no hint, and therefore before the first Assyrian
attack, to which there is no distinct reference. The series of
judgments culminates in the threat of Assyrian invasion
(v. 26–30). It is probable that this final threat alone is strictly
predictive, and that the other judgments, which leave the hand
of God still stretched out, are to be regarded as already past. A
similar series of past chastisements, also ending with a threat of
further judgment, is described in Amos iv. 6–12.
8. hath lighted: rather 'shall fall.' The word has been
sent through the prophet; its fulfilment is inevitable.
9. shall know: will experience the judgment, and recognize
that the word came from God.
10. The foolish bravado of Ephraim, blindly optimistic even
in the midst of losses and defeats. The words may be quoted
from a song actually current among the people. The reference

build with hewn stone: the sycomores are cut down, but
11 we will change them into cedars. Therefore the LORD
shall set up on high against him the adversaries of Rezin,
12 and shall stir up his enemies; the Syrians before, and
the Philistines behind; and they shall devour Israel with
open mouth. For all this his anger is not turned away,
but his hand is stretched out still.

13-17. *Judgment by decimation of the male population.*

13 Yet the people hath not turned unto him that smote
them, neither have they sought the LORD of hosts.
14 Therefore the LORD will cut off from Israel head and tail,
15 palm-branch and rush, in one day. The ancient and
the honourable man, he is the head; and the prophet
16 that teacheth lies, he is the tail. For they that lead this
people cause them to err; and they that are led of them
17 are destroyed. Therefore the Lord shall not rejoice over
their young men, neither shall he have compassion on

is not to the attack by Assyria begun in 734, but to earlier
reverses in the frequent wars with Syria. For the reckless
optimism of Ephraim in the face of such defeats cf. Hos.
vii. 8-11.

11. shall set up...shall stir up : 'set up...stirred up.'

adversaries of Rezin. The king of Syria was himself one of
the adversaries, as *v.* 12 ('the Syrians') shows. Read 'his
adversary,' and regard 'Rezin' as a gloss.

12. shall devour : 'devoured.' To what event reference is
made is uncertain. It is not clear that any particular campaign
was in the prophet's mind. The language is general and does
not necessarily imply a concerted attack by Syrians and Philistines.

For...still. This impressive conception dominates the entire
poem. Yahwe's hand is stretched out in judgment, and is not
withdrawn until the final catastrophe is reached (v. 26-30).

14. will cut off : 'cut off.'

head...rush. The blow fell on high and low alike, probably
in some sanguinary defeat.

15. A gloss, giving an incorrect explanation of the proverbial
expressions in *v.* 14.

17. rejoice over: i.e. 'take pleasure in' or 'show favour to';
but the conjecture 'spare' gives better sense.

their fatherless and widows: for every one is profane and
an evildoer, and every mouth speaketh folly. For all this
his anger is not turned away, but his hand is stretched
out still.

18-21. *Judgment by desolation and anarchy.*

For wickedness burneth as the fire; it devoureth the 18
briers and thorns: yea, it kindleth in the thickets of the
forest, and they roll upward in thick clouds of smoke.
Through the wrath of the LORD of hosts is the land 19
burnt up: the people also are as the fuel of fire; no man
spareth his brother. And one shall snatch on the right 20
hand, and be hungry; and he shall eat on the left hand,
and they shall not be satisfied: they shall eat every man
the flesh of his own arm: Manasseh, Ephraim; and 21
Ephraim, Manasseh: and they together shall be against
Judah. For all this his anger is not turned away, but his
hand is stretched out still.

x. 1-4. *A denunciation of unjust and oppressive legislation.*

Woe unto them that decree unrighteous decrees, and to **10**
the writers that write perverseness: to turn aside the 2
needy from judgement, and to take away the right of the
poor of my people, that widows may be their spoil, and

18, 19. The unrepentant wickedness of the people is like a
forest fire which, starting among the thorns, mounts up till it
consumes the trees. Not only is the land desolate, but the
people also are consumed the one by the other.

19. are...fire : the context justifies an easy emendation to
' became like man-eaters.'

20, 21. The future tenses should be past. The verses portray
anarchy and internecine strife and jealousy. How long the
ancient jealousies and frictions of the various tribes survived is
not known. The tribal names may be used here typically of
strife between brothers and between factions in the state.

20. of his own arm : read ' of his neighbour'; cf. Jer. xix. 9.

x. 1, 2. The abuse of judicial power is a frequent subject of
prophetic denunciation. Here the reference is to written enact-
ments on which unjust decisions might be based.

3 that they may make the fatherless their prey! And what
will ye do in the day of visitation, and in the desolation
which shall come from far? to whom will ye flee for
4 help? and where will ye leave your glory? They shall
only bow down under the prisoners, and shall fall under
the slain. For all this his anger is not turned away, but
his hand is stretched out still.

5–xii. *The overthrow of the Assyrian Empire, and the
establishment of the Messianic kingdom.*

x. 5–34. *The Divine judgment on Assyria.*

5 Ho Assyrian, the rod of mine anger, the staff in whose
6 hand is mine indignation! I will send him against a profane nation, and against the people of my wrath will I give

---

3. what...visitation: cf. Hos. ix. 5–7.

desolation [rather 'storm']...**far.** The first hint of the
Assyrian peril; cf. v. 26.

glory: i.e. treasures.

4. The text is corrupt and unintelligible. The sense seems
to be 'you will have no resource except to bow...and fall.' The
ingenious emendation 'Belti bows down, Osiris is broken' leaves
the verse still awkward, and presupposes a more widely diffused
cult of Egyptian deities in Israel at that period than we are
justified in assuming.

For the conclusion of the poem see v. 25 ff.

VI. Ch. x. 5–xii. 8.

5–34. Assyria is Yahwe's instrument for the punishment of His
people, and derives its power from Him. But in its arrogance
it cherishes ambitious schemes of conquest, and derides the
majesty of Yahwe, imagining that its successes are due to its
own might. It will make an attack on Jerusalem, but Yahwe
will destroy its power, and deliver the Remnant of His people.

The date of the passage is between 717 (the fall of Carchemish, *v.* 9) and 701 (the destruction of Sennacherib's army).
It is not clear that the whole oracle was delivered at one time,
nor is it necessary to suppose that it was called forth by any
specific event, such as the campaign of Sargon in 711. The
most suitable date is shortly before the crisis of 701.

5. the staff...indignation: read 'and the staff of my
indignation.'

6. I will send: rather 'I am sending.'

him a charge, to take the spoil, and to take the prey, and
to tread them down like the mire of the streets. Howbeit 7
he meaneth not so, neither doth his heart think so; but
it is in his heart to destroy, and to cut off nations not a
few. For he saith, Are not my princes all of them kings? 8
Is not Calno as Carchemish? is not Hamath as Arpad? 9
is not Samaria as Damascus? As my hand hath found 10
the kingdoms of the idols, whose graven images did excel
them of Jerusalem and of Samaria; shall I not, as I have 11
done unto Samaria and her idols, so do to Jerusalem and
her idols?

Wherefore it shall come to pass, that when the Lord 12
hath performed his whole work upon mount Zion and on
Jerusalem, I will punish the fruit of the stout heart of the
king of Assyria, and the glory of his high looks. For he 13
hath said, By the strength of my hand I have done it,
and by my wisdom; for I am prudent: and I have removed the bounds of the peoples, and have robbed their

---

7. Assyria has no intention of being the instrument of the
execution of Yahwe's purpose, but contemplates its own aggran-
disement and the extinction of many nationalities.

8. princes : rather 'officers,' the governors of conquered
provinces, like the Persian satraps. Some of these governors
were conquered kings, now vassals of the Assyrian 'king of
kings.'

9. Six cities are enumerated in three pairs, each pair bringing
the limit of conquest nearer to Jerusalem. Carchemish, Jerabis
on the Euphrates, fell in 717, Calno, possibly Kullani in North
Syria, in 738, Arpad, near Aleppo, in 740, and again, after an
insurrection, along with Hamath, in 720, Damascus in 732, and
Samaria in 722/1.

10. found : marg. 'reached,' i.e. 'taken possession of,' as
in *v.* 14.

idols : 'nonentities,' as in ii. 8.

whose...images : 'though their graven images....'

12. The interruption of the speech of the Assyrian king is
probably interpolated.

I will punish : LXX reads 'He will punish,' but the sudden
change of person is not without parallel; e.g. xxii. 18, 19.

13. I have...peoples. Incorporation in the Assyrian Empire
robbed the old frontiers of significance, and the deportation of

treasures, and I have brought down as a valiant man
14 them that sit *on thrones*: and my hand hath found as a
nest the riches of the peoples; and as one gathereth eggs
that are forsaken, have I gathered all the earth: and
there was none that moved the wing, or that opened the
15 mouth, or chirped.   Shall the axe boast itself against him
that heweth therewith? shall the saw magnify itself against
him that shaketh it? as if a rod should shake them that lift
it up, *or* as if a staff should lift up *him that is* not wood.

16   Therefore shall the Lord, the LORD of hosts, send
among his fat ones leanness; and under his glory there
17 shall be kindled a burning like the burning of fire.   And
the light of Israel shall be for a fire, and his Holy One
for a flame: and it shall burn and devour his thorns and
18 his briers in one day.   And he shall consume the glory
of his forest, and of his fruitful field, both soul and body:
19 and it shall be as when a standardbearer fainteth.   And
the remnant of the trees of his forest shall be few, that a
child may write them.

---

whole populations tended to extinguish national unity and
sentiment.

brought...thrones.   The text is corrupt, and no satisfactory
emendation has been suggested.

14.   A fine image of unresisted conquest.

15. him that is not wood: lit. 'not-wood,' i.e. a man, in
contrast to the staff he wields.

16–19.   Two images of the destruction of the Assyrians:—
disease, *vv.* 16*a*, 18*b*; and a forest fire, *vv.* 16*b*–18*a*, 19.   The
mingling of the metaphors is very awkward, and may have
arisen when the various sayings or addresses of which the
passage is composed were pieced together.

16. among...leanness: rather 'upon his well-nourished limbs
a wasting sickness.'

17.   Cf. ix. 18.   'The light of Israel' (parallel to 'his Holy
One') means Yahwe.

18. soul and body: an abrupt change of metaphor, apparently intended to lead up to the resumption of the figure of
sickness in the next clause.

when...fainteth: read 'when a sick man pineth away.'

19. write them: i.e. make a list of them.

And it shall come to pass in that day, that the 20
remnant of Israel, and they that are escaped of the house
of Jacob, shall no more again stay upon him that smote
them ; but shall stay upon the LORD, the Holy One of
Israel, in truth. A remnant shall return, *even* the 21
remnant of Jacob, unto the mighty God. For though 22
thy people Israel be as the sand of the sea, *only* a remnant
of them shall return : a consumption *is* determined, overflowing with righteousness. For a consummation, and 23
that determined, shall the Lord, the LORD of hosts, make
in the midst of all the earth.

Therefore thus saith the Lord, the LORD of hosts, O 24
my people that dwellest in Zion, be not afraid of the

20-23. The salvation of the Remnant.

These verses, though possibly Isaiah's, are unsuitably placed,
and can hardly have been the original continuation of *vv.*
16-19, which proclaim the destruction of the Assyrians, and
are followed naturally by *vv.* 24-27, an exhortation to quiet
confidence in Yahwe and a further threat against Assyria.
Vv. 20-23, on the other hand, threaten Judah with almost
complete destruction, and emphasize the numerical insignificance
of the Remnant.

20. shall no more...Lord. An allusion to the policy of Ahaz
in making himself tributary to Assyria in order to purchase
Assyrian help against Syria and North Israel (see on vii. 1-17).
There is no evidence that Hezekiah, who had to reap the bitter
fruit of that policy, himself relied in any way on Assyria. But
the main point is the contrast between dependence on a foreign
power, working for its own ends, and reliance on Yahwe 'in
truth,' i.e. in loyalty to Him.

21. remnant...return : see on vii. 3.

mighty God : 'Hero-God,' as in ix. 6, where, however, the
reference is not to Yahwe, but to the Messianic king.

22. Israel : vocative, ' O Israel.'

consumption is determined : rather 'extermination is decreed.'

overflowing with righteousness. The extermination of the
great mass of the people will be an exhibition on a grand scale
of the judicial righteousness of God.

23. For...determined, shall...make : ' For an extermination
and a fixed decree shall...execute.' The 'fixed decree' is a
decisive manifestation of the Divine purpose.

24. The continuation of *v.* 19. (See on *vv.* 20-23.)

Assyrian: though he smite thee with the rod, and lift up
25 his staff against thee, after the manner of Egypt. For yet a
very little while, and the indignation shall be accomplished,
26 and mine anger, in their destruction. And the LORD of
hosts shall stir up against him a scourge, as in the slaughter
of Midian at the rock of Oreb : and his rod shall be over
the sea, and he shall lift it up after the manner of Egypt.
27 And it shall come to pass in that day, that his burden
shall depart from off thy shoulder, and his yoke from off
thy neck, and the yoke shall be destroyed because of the
anointing.

---

though he smite...and lift : rather ' who smites...and lifts.'

after...Egypt : i.e. as Egypt smote in the ancient days of
bondage.

25. and mine...destruction : 'and mine anger is for (i.e. is
directed to) their (the Assyrians') destruction.' When the
punishment of Judah is accomplished the Divine wrath will be
turned against her foes. For the change in the number of the
pronouns—he...his...their—cf. *vv.* 28, 29.

26. stir...him : rather ' brandish over him,' as Abishai bran-
dished his spear, 2 Sam. xxiii. 18.

as...Oreb : cf. ix. 4 ; Jud. vii. 25.

and...Egypt : 'and his rod over the sea (i.e. the rod which was
once stretched over the sea, Ex. xiv. 16) shall he lift up after
the manner of Egypt,' i.e. as it was lifted up to destroy the
Egyptians : a striking antithesis to *v.* 24.

27. and...neck. The destruction of the Assyrians meant the
deliverance of Judah from the galling yoke of vassalage, which
had been upon her neck since Ahaz first paid tribute in 735/4.

and the yoke...anointing. The text is corrupt, and no
reasonable meaning can be extorted from it. The best conjectural emendation is to take the clause with the following
verse, and read ' he advances from Pene-Rimmon,' i.e. the
Rock Rimmon (Jud. xx. 45), somewhat east of Bethel and
north of Aiath.

28-34. A sketch of the possible route of an Assyrian expedi-
tion against Judah. The itinerary given, though geographically
accurate, is neither history nor prophecy, but an imaginative
description of what might be the manner and effect of the
Assyrian march up to the moment of the actual attack on
Jerusalem, when Yahwe would intervene to destroy the invaders.
The Assyrians followed another route in 702/1, and this passage
is therefore to be dated at a time when, though invasion was

He is come to Aiath, he is passed through Migron ; 28
at Michmash he layeth up his baggage : they are gone 29
over the pass ; they have taken up their lodging at Geba :
Ramah trembleth ; Gibeah of Saul is fled. Cry aloud 30
with thy voice, O daughter of Gallim ! hearken, O
Laishah ! O thou poor Anathoth ! Madmenah is a 31
fugitive ; the inhabitants of Gebim gather themselves to
flee. This very day shall he halt at Nob : he shaketh his 32
hand at the mount of the daughter of Zion, the hill of
Jerusalem.

Behold, the Lord, the LORD of hosts, shall lop the 33
boughs with terror : and the high ones of stature shall be

---

imminent, the precise point of attack was not yet certain. The
connection with the preceding verses is quite loose.

28. **He…Aiath** : read '[*v.* 27 *b*, he advances from Pene-
Rimmon,] he comes upon Aiath,' i.e. Ai (Jos. vii. 2 ; cf. also
1 Chron. vii. 28 marg. ; Neh. xi. 31), probably a short distance
S.E. of Bethel, though the site is uncertain.

he…Migron : 'he passes through Migron,' probably Makrun,
not far from Michmash.

29. Between Michmash (cf. 1 Sam. xiii., xiv.) and Geba lies
the **pass**, the Wady es-Suweinit, which at one point is a
narrow ravine between high cliffs. As a precaution against
confusion in the event of resistance in the pass the baggage is
temporarily left at Michmash.

they have…Geba : 'they make Geba their night-quarters,' a
more satisfactory rendering than marg. 'Geba is our lodging,'
an exclamation of the Assyrians.

Ramah, er-Ram, slightly S.W. of Geba ; **Gibeah of Saul**,
probably Tell el-Ful, about half-way between Geba and
Jerusalem.

30, 31. The sites of Gallim, Laishah, Madmenah, and Gebim
are unknown. Anathoth, the birthplace of Jeremiah, is Anata,
slightly S.E. of Tell el-Ful, and N.E. of Jerusalem.

30. O thou poor Anathoth : read 'Answer her, O Anathoth.'

32. Nob : cf. 1 Sam. xxi., xxii. The site is unknown, but
it was evidently quite near Jerusalem.

33, 34. At the last moment the blow falls on the invading
host. Yahwe lays them low as a woodman hews down the tall
trees of a forest.

33. with terror : read 'with the axe,' parallel to 'with
iron,' *v.* 34.

34 hewn down, and the lofty shall be brought low. And he
shall cut down the thickets of the forest with iron, and
Lebanon shall fall by a mighty one.

xi. 1–9. *The Messiah and his reign of peace.*

11 And there shall come forth a shoot out of the stock of
2 Jesse, and a branch out of his roots shall bear fruit: and
the spirit of the LORD shall rest upon him, the spirit of
wisdom and understanding, the spirit of counsel and
might, the spirit of knowledge and of the fear of the
3 LORD; and his delight shall be in the fear of the LORD:
and he shall not judge after the sight of his eyes, neither
4 reprove after the hearing of his ears: but with righteous-

---

34. mighty one: i.e. Yahwe. The expression is peculiar,
and the reading 'Lebanon shall fall with its cedars' is on the
whole preferable.

xi. 1–9. The prediction of the deliverance of Jerusalem and the
Divine judgment on the Assyrians is followed immediately and
naturally by a figurative delineation of the peace and prosperity
of the Messiah's reign.

1. stock of Jesse. The image is that of a stump, left in the
ground after a tree has been felled, the roots of which are sound,
so that there is hope of new growth; cf. vi. 13. The reference
to Jesse may imply that the existing Davidic dynasty will perish,
and that from some remaining 'stock' of the ancient family a
new royal line will spring. But the language is vague and may
mean no more than that the Messianic king will be like David,
who was the first great shoot from the stock of Jesse.

2. The Spirit of Yahwe will endow the Messianic king
with every needed grace and virtue, intellectual, practical, and
spiritual. With the qualities here ascribed to him compare the
list of Messianic titles in ix. 6.

3. his delight...Lord: lit. 'his scent shall be for the fear of
Yahwe,' i.e. he will unfailingly and joyfully recognize true piety
in others. But this is a dubious interpretation of a strange
expression, and the clause should perhaps be read 'He (i.e.
Yahwe) will cause the fear of Yahwe to rest upon him,' and be
regarded as a gloss to the preceding words.

and he...ears: i.e. he will not judge by external evidence
merely, but will read the hearts of men.

reprove: render 'decide' here and in *v.* 4.

ness shall he judge the poor, and reprove with equity for
the meek of the earth: and he shall smite the earth with
the rod of his mouth, and with the breath of his lips shall
he slay the wicked. And righteousness shall be the 5
girdle of his loins, and faithfulness the girdle of his reins.
And the wolf shall dwell with the lamb, and the leopard 6
shall lie down with the kid ; and the calf and the young lion
and the fatling together; and a little child shall lead them.
And the cow and the bear shall feed ; their young ones 7
shall lie down together: and the lion shall eat straw
like the ox. And the sucking child shall play on the hole 8
of the asp, and the weaned child shall put his hand on the
basilisk's den. They shall not hurt nor destroy in all my 9
holy mountain : for the earth shall be full of the knowledge
of the LORD, as the waters cover the sea.

---

4. meek of the earth: render 'the down-trodden in the
land.'

smite the earth : read 'smite the oppressor.'

It is noteworthy that violence and oppression are not regarded
as immediately and totally ceasing on the establishment of the
Messianic kingdom. They may exist, but they are sternly and
effectually repressed.

5. faithfulness the girdle : cf. the 'girdle of truth,'
Eph. vi. 14. The girdle braces up the wearer to vigorous
and resolute action.

6-9. An imaginative description of the peace and security
enjoyed under the Messianic rule. Harmony prevails throughout the whole creation, and beasts of prey lose their predatory
and destructive instincts.

8. The asp and basilisk are species of deadly serpents, though
they cannot be certainly identified with species known to have
existed in Palestine.

9. The pronoun is indefinite, and does not refer particularly
to the wild beasts.

all...mountain. The mountain is Zion, the holy seat of
Yahwe and the Messiah, but by a natural extension the expression practically means the whole extent of the Messianic
kingdom.

10-16. *The ingathering of the scattered Remnant
in the Messianic age.*

10 And it shall come to pass in that day, that the root of
Jesse, which standeth for an ensign of the peoples, unto
him shall the nations seek ; and his resting place shall be
glorious.

11 And it shall come to pass in that day, that the Lord
shall set his hand again the second time to recover the
remnant of his people, which shall remain, from Assyria,
and from Egypt, and from Pathros, and from Cush, and
from Elam, and from Shinar, and from Hamath, and
12 from the islands of the sea. And he shall set up an
ensign for the nations, and shall assemble the outcasts of
Israel, and gather together the dispersed of Judah from
13 the four corners of the earth. The envy also of Ephraim
shall depart, and they that vex Judah shall be cut off:

10-16. This passage is probably post-exilic. There is a Jewish
diaspora in many lands, and a second restoration is anticipated,
recalling, on the most natural interpretation of *v.* 11, the return
from the Babylonian captivity.

10. An isolated verse depicting the widespread spiritual influence of the 'root of Jesse,' i.e. the sprout from the root
(cf. liii. 2), apparently in later times a recognized title of the
Messiah.

11-16. Military and political successes of the restored people.

11. again...time : a reference possibly to the Exodus as in
v. 16, but more probably to the return from Babylon. Transl.
'Yahwe will again lift up his hand to recover...,' substituting
the word for 'lift up' for 'the second time.'

Assyria. The use of the name, applied to the dominant
power in Western Asia, survived after the real Assyrians had
lost their empire. Cf. Ezra vi. 22.

Pathros (Upper Egypt) and **Cush** (Ethiopia) were depen-
dencies of Egypt. **Elam** (Susiana), **Shinar** (Babylonia) and
Hamath (see x. 9) belonged successively to the Assyrian,
Babylonian, and Persian Empires.

13. The cessation not only of foreign oppression, but also of
internecine rivalry and conflict. The ancient jealousies of the
two kingdoms reappeared in the relations between Jerusalem and
Samaria after the Exile.

they that vex Judah : strict parallelism requires the sense

Ephraim shall not envy Judah, and Judah shall not vex
Ephraim. And they shall fly down upon the shoulder of 14
the Philistines on the west ; together shall they spoil the
children of the east : they shall put forth their hand upon
Edom and Moab ; and the children of Ammon shall
obey them. And the LORD shall utterly destroy the 15
tongue of the Egyptian sea ; and with his scorching wind
shall he shake his hand over the River, and shall smite it
into seven streams, and cause men to march over dryshod.
And there shall be an high way for the remnant of his 16
people, which shall remain, from Assyria ; like as there
was for Israel in the day that he came up out of the land
of Egypt.

xii. *Two brief hymns of praise to be sung by the restored people.*

And in that day thou shalt say, I will give thanks unto **12**
thee, O LORD; for though thou wast angry with me, thine
anger is turned away, and thou comfortest me. Behold, 2
God is my salvation ; I will trust, and will not be afraid :
for the LORD JEHOVAH is my strength and song ; and he

'they in Judah that oppress (Ephraim)' ; but it is perhaps
better to retain R.V. translation, and regard the parallelism as
defective.

14. shoulder : the slope of the Philistine territory from the
Judaean mountains to the sea. Cf. Num. xxxiv. 11 marg.

15. destroy : read 'dry up,' a reminiscence of the passage of
the Red Sea, the **tongue** of which is the gulf of Suez.

the River: the Euphrates (vii. 20, viii. 7), which will be split
up into seven shallow streams, so that men may cross it **dryshod**
(lit. in sandals).

16. For the idea of a 'highway' for the return of the exiles
cf. xl. 3 f., xlii. 16 etc.

xii. A liturgical appendix to ch. i.–xi., connected by the
opening formula with the immediately preceding oracle. The
two poems (*vv.* 1, 2, and *vv.* 4–6) are post-exilic, and consist
largely of reminiscences of Ex. xv., parts of ch. xxiv.–xxvii.,
and certain Psalms.

1. God...salvation : rather 'the God of my salvation.'

2. the Lord Jehovah : read simply 'Yah,' a rarer form of
'Yahwe'; cf. Ex. xv. 2 marg.

3 is become my salvation. Therefore with joy shall ye
4 draw water out of the wells of salvation. And in that
   day shall ye say, Give thanks unto the LORD, call upon
   his name, declare his doings among the peoples, make
5 mention that his name is exalted. Sing unto the LORD;
   for he hath done excellent things: let this be known in
6 all the earth. Cry aloud and shout, thou inhabitant of
   Zion: for great is the Holy One of Israel in the midst of
   thee.

xiii.   *The impending fall of Babylon.*

13   The burden of Babylon, which Isaiah the son of Amoz
       did see.

2-4.   *The mustering of Yahwe's hosts.*

2   Set ye up an ensign upon the bare mountain, lift up
     the voice unto them, wave the hand, that they may go

---

3. A promise introducing the second song *vv.* 4–6.
wells of salvation : cf. lv. 1 ; Jer. ii. 13 ; Ps. lxxxvii. 7.
4. call...name: i.e. call Him by His name (in worship).
Cf. Ps. cv. 1.

Ch. xiii.–xxiii. A SERIES OF PROPHECIES RELATING CHIEFLY TO FOREIGN NATIONS.

I. Ch. xiii.–xiv. 23.

An oracle on Babylon and her king.

The historical situation is that of the closing years of the exile,
and the passage is therefore to be assigned to that date. It
consists of two poems, xiii. 2–22 and xiv. 4 *b*–21. xiii. 1 and
xiv. 1–4 *a* are editorial, and xiv. 22, 23 form a brief epilogue.
   With this poem cf. Jer. l., li.
   xiii. 1. burden: 'the lifting up (of the voice),' especially when
speaking in the name of God, so 'oracle.' The word occurs 10
times in editorial superscriptions in ch. xiii.–xxiii., and also in
xxx. 6, but never in genuine writings of Isaiah. The meaning
'burden' is applied to it scornfully in Jer. xxiii. 33–40.
   did see: see on ii. 1.
   2. bare mountain : a treeless summit, so that a signal on it
might be easily seen.

into the gates of the nobles. I have commanded my 3
consecrated ones, yea, I have called my mighty men for
mine anger, even my proudly exulting ones. The noise 4
of a multitude in the mountains, like as of a great people!
the noise of a tumult of the kingdoms of the nations
gathered together! the LORD of hosts mustereth the host
for the battle.

5-8. *Terror and dismay in the city.*

They come from a far country, from the uttermost part of 5
heaven, even the LORD, and the weapons of his indignation, to destroy the whole land. Howl ye; for the day of 6
the LORD is at hand; as destruction from the Almighty
shall it come. Therefore shall all hands be feeble, and 7
every heart of man shall melt: and they shall be dismayed; 8
pangs and sorrows shall take hold *of them*; they shall be
in pain as a woman in travail: they shall be amazed
one at another; their faces *shall be* faces of flame.

9-12. *The Day of Yahwe, a day of awful destruction.*

Behold, the day of the LORD cometh, cruel, with wrath 9
and fierce anger; to make the land a desolation, and to

---

gates...nobles: the gates of Babylon, the imperial city.
Babylon itself (Bab-ilu) means 'gate of God.'

3. Yahwe speaks.

consecrated ones: an army mustered by Yahwe for the
carrying out of His purposes; cf. Jer. xxii. 7 marg. It was
customary to offer sacrifices at the commencement of a campaign
(1 Sam. xiii. 9), and the Israelites, like the neighbouring peoples,
regarded their God as Himself leading them in battle (Ex. xv. 3;
Deut. xxiii. 14).

4. The...mountains: 'Hark! a tumult in the mountains,' i.e.
the Median mountains, from which the Medo-Persian army
descended upon Babylon.

5. land: rather 'earth,' i.e. the Babylonian Empir
regarded as practically embracing the world.

6. Cf. Joel i. 15.

day of the Lord: see on ii. 12.

8. they shall be amazed one at another: rather 'they
stare at each other' (in horror and dismay).

their...flame: their faces are flushed with feverish anxiety.

10 destroy the sinners thereof out of it. For the stars of
heaven and the constellations thereof shall not give their
light: the sun shall be darkened in his going forth, and
11 the moon shall not cause her light to shine. And I will
punish the world for *their* evil, and the wicked for their
iniquity; and I will cause the arrogancy of the proud to
cease, and will lay low the haughtiness of the terrible.
12 I will make a man more rare than fine gold, even a man
than the pure gold of Ophir.

13–16. *Flight and massacre.*

13 Therefore I will make the heavens to tremble, and the
earth shall be shaken out of her place, in the wrath of
the LORD of hosts, and in the day of his fierce anger.
14 And it shall come to pass, that as the chased roe, and as
sheep that no man gathereth, they shall turn every man
to his own people, and shall flee every man to his own
15 land. Every one that is found shall be thrust through;
16 and every one that is taken shall fall by the sword. Their
infants also shall be dashed in pieces before their eyes;
their houses shall be spoiled, and their wives ravished.

---

10.   Darkness and gloom were characteristic features of the
'Day of Yahwe' as pictured by the prophets; cf. Amos v. 18;
Zeph. i. 15.

constellations: lit. 'Orions' (cf. Amos v. 8), the plural
meaning, in effect, the great constellations like Orion.

11.   Yahwe again speaks, as in *v.* 3.

the terrible: rather 'the tyrants.'

12.   A threat of almost complete extermination.

Ophir (Gen. x. 29; 1 Kings ix. 28): probably on the S.E.
coast of Arabia.

13.   I...tremble: read 'the heavens shall tremble.' Yahwe
is not the speaker in *vv.* 13–16.

14.   The foreigners who have crowded into Babylon in the
great days of her imperial and commercial prosperity will be
scattered like sheep with no shepherd to keep them together.

15, 16.   The terrible fate of the Babylonians, who have no
other land to which to flee.

These anticipations, however, were not realized, as the actual
victors displayed the greatest possible clemency.

*17–19. The Medes are named as the instruments of
Yahwe's wrath.*

Behold, I will stir up the Medes against them, which shall 17
not regard silver, and as for gold, they shall not delight
in it.   And *their* bows shall dash the young men in 18
pieces; and they shall have no pity on the fruit of the
womb; their eye shall not spare children.   And Babylon, 19
the glory of kingdoms, the beauty of the Chaldeans' pride,
shall be as when God overthrew Sodom and Gomorrah.

20–22. The utter desolation of Babylonia.

It shall never be inhabited, neither shall it be dwelt in 20
from generation to generation : neither shall the Arabian
pitch tent there; neither shall shepherds make their

---

17. Yahwe Himself speaks once more.
Medes. The power of Assyria was finally broken (B.C. 606) by
the Babylonians, with the aid of the Medes, who obtained a
share of the spoil, and established themselves as the second
power in Asia.   About B.C. 550 Cyrus, king of Anzan, in
Elam, and Persia, at that time an unimportant state, over-
came Astyages, king of Media, and took possession of his
throne.   He began immediately to extend his empire, and,
having conquered Lydia, proceeded to attack Babylon, which
fell in 538.   In later times the Medo-Persian Empire, thus
founded and extended, was generally called Persian.   But the
name 'Median' survived in common use for a long period, and.
is employed by most Greek writers.   In such late works as
Esther and Daniel the names are still used side by side, Esth.
i. 3 ; Dan. v. 28.   Whether, therefore, this passage was written
before or after the rise of Cyrus to supreme power, the conquering host would naturally be described as Median.
which...it : no bribe or tribute could stop the Median
advance.
18.   bows : the characteristic Persian weapon.
19.   Chaldeans : Chaldaea proper lay S.E. of Babylonia,
near the head of the Persian Gulf.   Nabopalassar (c. 626 B.C.),
father of Nebuchadnezzar, was a Chaldaean, and his conquests
made Chaldaea and Babylonia practically synonymous terms.
overthrew Sodom : see on i. 7.

21 flocks to lie down there.　But wild beasts of the desert
shall lie there; and their houses shall be full of doleful
creatures; and ostriches shall dwell there, and satyrs
22 shall dance there.　And wolves shall cry in their castles,
and jackals in the pleasant palaces: and her time is near
to come, and her days shall not be prolonged.

xiv. 1-4 *a.　The restoration of Israel.*

14　For the LORD will have compassion on Jacob, and will
yet choose Israel, and set them in their own land: and the
stranger shall join himself with them, and they shall cleave
2 to the house of Jacob.　And the peoples shall take them,
and bring them to their place: and the house of Israel
shall possess them in the land of the LORD for servants
and for handmaids: and they shall take them captive,
whose captives they were; and they shall rule over their
oppressors.

3　And it shall come to pass in the day that the LORD
shall give thee rest from thy sorrow, and from thy trouble,
and from the hard service wherein thou wast made to
4 serve, that thou shalt take up this parable against the
king of Babylon, and say,

21.　**doleful creatures**: lit. 'howlers,' possibly jackals.
　　satyrs: lit. 'hairy ones,' goat-shaped demons, that haunted
waste and desolate spots.
22.　**wolves...jackals**: what animals are meant is uncertain.
Their howling echoes through the ruined halls, while the satyrs
dance.
　　xiv. 1-4 *a.*　A prose insertion connecting the two poems.
Israel will be restored, and will become master of the heathen
peoples instead of their servant, triumphing especially over the
nation that had enslaved him.
　　1.　**the stranger**: proselytes who would attach themselves
permanently to Israel.
　　2.　For the idea of Israel's lordship over the heathen peoples
cf. lx. 10-16, lxi. 5.
　　4.　**parable**: rather 'taunt-song.' The word for parable, or
proverb, a gnomic saying often containing a similitude, acquired
the secondary meaning of a sarcastic ode; cf. Num. xxi. 27;
Hab. ii. 6.

4 b–21. The fate of the king of Babylon.

4 b–8. The relief and joy of the world at the fall of the tyrant.

How hath the oppressor ceased! the golden city ceased!
The LORD hath broken the staff of the wicked, the 5
sceptre of the rulers; that smote the peoples in wrath 6
with a continual stroke, that ruled the nations in anger,
with a persecution that none restrained.   The whole 7
earth is at rest, *and* is quiet: they break forth into
singing.   Yea, the fir trees rejoice at thee, *and* the cedars 8
of Lebanon, *saying*, Since thou art laid down, no feller is
come up against us.

9–11. The agitation of Sheol at the approach of the king.

Hell from beneath is moved for thee to meet thee at thy 9
coming: it stirreth up the dead for thee, even all the
chief ones of the earth; it hath raised up from their

---

4 b–21. An ironical dirge, in the Ḳinah rhythm (see on i. 21),
falling into five regular strophes, each of seven double lines.
The sombre grandeur of the poem is unsurpassed in Hebrew
literature.

4. ceased : rather 'been stilled.'

golden city : read 'arrogant rage.'

6. that ruled...restrained : rather 'that mastered the nations
in anger, with unrestrained mastery.'

8. Since...us. Assyrian and Babylonian rulers frequently
robbed the forests of Lebanon in order to provide materials for
their great buildings and for military purposes.

9. Hell : 'Sheol,' or Hades, the underworld of shades.
With the description of this underworld in *vv.* 9–20 cf. Ez.
xxxii. 17 ff. The dead are shadowy, bloodless creatures, with
little power of movement, who can, however, be roused to
take at least a passing interest in some exceptionally important
event, such as the fall of an empire, or the advent among themselves of a great king. The fate of the body after death has a
certain influence upon the condition of the shade in the lower
world, *vv.* 9, 11, 18 f., and exceptional wickedness may cause
the corpse to be dishonoured, *v.* 20. Otherwise there is no
trace of reward or punishment in Sheol.

it hath...nations. The kings who have received honourable
burial continue to sit on thrones even in Sheol. Cf. the Greek

10 thrones all the kings of the nations. All they shall answer
   and say unto thee, Art thou also become weak as we? art
11 thou become like unto us? Thy pomp is brought down
   to hell, *and* the noise of thy viols: the worm is spread
   under thee, and worms cover thee.

   12–15. *The pride that soared to heaven is humbled to the abyss.*

12 How art thou fallen from heaven, O day star, son of the
   morning! how art thou cut down to the ground, which
13 didst lay low the nations! And thou saidst in thine heart,
   I will ascend into heaven, I will exalt my throne above
   the stars of God; and I will sit upon the mount of
14 congregation, in the uttermost parts of the north: I will
   ascend above the heights of the clouds; I will be like
15 the Most High. Yet thou shalt be brought down to hell,
   to the uttermost parts of the pit.

   16–19. *The astonishment and derision of those who see
   the king's unburied corpse.*

16 They that see thee shall narrowly look upon thee, they shall
   consider thee, *saying*, Is this the man that made the earth

---

idea of the influence upon the shades of their occupations and
interests when alive.

11. the worm...thee. The dishonoured king has no throne
in Sheol; his bed is corruption, and his covering the worms.

12. day star...morning. The king in his glory is compared
to Lucifer, the morning star, Son of the Dawn. Not content
with this position of pre-eminence among his peers, he aspires
to divine honours (*vv.* 13, 14), and falls from his exalted place.

13. mount...north. The mysterious mountain of the gods,
a conception resembling that of the Greek Olympus, was placed
by the Indians and Persians, and, as this verse indicates, by
the Babylonians also, in the extreme north. A trace of this
conception is found in Ps. xlviii. 3, where the same phrase 'in
the recesses of the north' is metaphorically applied to Zion.

14. I...like... : rather 'I will make myself like....'

15. Read 'thou shalt be cast down to Sheol, to the recesses
of the pit' (= Sheol), a striking contrast to the divine mountain
'in the recesses of the north.'

16 ff. The text of *vv.* 16–21 is in some confusion, and the correct
rhythm can be restored only by conjectural emendation. The

to tremble, that did shake kingdoms; that made the world 17
as a wilderness, and overthrew the cities thereof; that let
not loose his prisoners to their home? All the kings of 18
the nations, all of them, sleep in glory, every one in his
own house. But thou art cast forth away from thy 19
sepulchre like an abominable branch, clothed with the
slain, that are thrust through with the sword, that go down
to the stones of the pit; as a carcase trodden under foot.

20, 21. *The extermination of the whole royal house.*

Thou shalt not be joined with them in burial, because 20
thou hast destroyed thy land, thou hast slain thy people;
the seed of evil-doers shall not be named for ever.
Prepare ye slaughter for his children for the iniquity of 21
their fathers; that they rise not up, and possess the earth,
and fill the face of the world with cities.

---

fourth strophe, *vv.* 16–19, is too long, and the fifth, *vv.* 20, 21,
too short. The exact sense of *vv.* 19, 20, is also uncertain.

17 *b*, 18. Read 'that let not loose his prisoners, each to his
home. The kings of the nations, all of them, sleep in honour.'

19. away...sepulchre: i.e., if the text be right, 'without
burial.'

clothed...slain: the slain covering him like a garment. (But
see next note.)

that go...pit. In its present context the phrase (or some
conjectural modification of it) must mean that those who fall by
the sword and are unburied go down to the lowest region of
Sheol, and this is the most natural interpretation. See on *vv.* 9,
11, and cf. Ez. xxxii. 21–32. The words 'away...clothed' disturb both rhythm and sense, and should be transferred to the
next strophe, as parallel to *v.* 20 *a*, though no satisfactory restoration of them has been suggested. Read here simply 'but thou
art cast forth with the slain that...' A less probable conjecture
is to transfer 'that go...pit' to the beginning of *v.* 20, taking the
words to mean honourable burial in a stone mausoleum.

20. Thou...burial. The first half-line is too short, and the
reference of the pronoun 'them' to the kings, *v.* 18, is very
awkward. Presumably the antecedent, possibly 'thy fathers,'
has dropped out.

21. slaughter: marg. 'place of slaughter.'

with cities: omit, as being unsuitable in sense, and rhythmi-
cally superfluous.

22, 23.   The epilogue.   A final threat of destruction.

22 And I will rise up against them, saith the LORD of hosts,
and cut off from Babylon name and remnant, and son and
23 son's son, saith the LORD.   I will also make it a possession
for the porcupine, and pools of water: and I will sweep
it with the besom of destruction, saith the LORD of hosts.

*24-27.   Yahwe's purpose to break the power of Assyria
in His land.*

The LORD of hosts hath sworn, saying, Surely as I
24 have thought, so shall it come to pass; and as I have
purposed, so shall it stand : that I will break the Assyrian
25 in my land, and upon my mountains tread him under foot :
then shall his yoke depart from off them, and his burden
depart from off their shoulder.   This is the purpose that
26 is purposed upon the whole earth: and this is the hand
that is stretched out upon all the nations.   For the LORD
27 of hosts hath purposed, and who shall disannul it? and
his hand is stretched out, and who shall turn it back?

---

23. porcupine : so LXX and other ancient versions. But
many scholars prefer A.V. rendering 'bittern' as more suitable
to the 'pools of water,' or marshes of the Euphrates valley.

II. Ch. xiv. 24-27.

A fragment of Isaianic prophecy to be dated shortly before
the destruction of Sennacherib's army, B.C. 701. Cf. x. 5 ff.
25. then...shoulder : cf. ix. 4, x. 27.
26. purpose...nations.   The Divine sovereignty is world-
wide, and consequently the Divine purpose affects the whole
earth.   Neither the political nor the religious consequences of
Yahwe's intervention against the Assyrians, whose power and
ambition embraced Isaiah's world, could therefore be restricted
to Israel.
hand...stretched out : cf. the refrain (ix. 12 etc.) of the
oracle against Ephraim, ix. 8-x. 4, v. 25-30.

28-32. *An oracle on Philistia.*

In the year that king Ahaz died was this burden.   28

Rejoice not, O Philistia, all of thee, because the rod 29
that smote thee is broken: for out of the serpent's root
shall come forth a basilisk, and his fruit shall be a fiery
flying serpent. And the firstborn of the poor shall feed, 30
and the needy shall lie down in safety: and I will kill thy
root with famine, and thy remnant shall be slain. Howl, 31
O gate; cry, O city; thou art melted away, O Philistia,
all of thee; for there ·cometh a smoke out of the north,
and none standeth aloof at his appointed times. What 32
then shall one answer the messengers of the nation?

III. Ch. xiv. 28-32.

The Philistines, imagining that the moment is opportune for
shaking off a foreign yoke, presumably that of Assyria, have
sent envoys to Jerusalem, probably to propose a concerted revolt.
In this oracle they are warned that their hopes are delusive, and
Judah is advised to decline their overtures, and reply that its
reliance is on Yahwe.

The date is uncertain, as *v.* 28 is probably editorial, and in any
case the year of Ahaz' death has not been certainly determined.
The occasion of the embassy was probably the death of an
Assyrian king (see on *v.* 29), and the confident tone in which the
security of Zion is spoken of, being characteristic of Isaiah's later
work, suggests 705 B.C., the year of the death of Sargon, and
the accession of Sennacherib.

29. The reference is to the death of a king who will be
succeeded by one of the same stock, still more powerful and
ruthless than himself. The reference to the north (*v.* 31)
indicates that an Assyrian king is meant.

fiery flying serpent: see on vi. 2.

30. the firstborn...poor: i.e. the very poorest. Read, however, 'in my meadow'—or 'on my mountains' (cf. *v.* 25)—'the
poor shall feed.'

the poor...needy: those who in humility and obedience put
their trust in Yahwe (cf. *v.* 32).

31. thou...away: render 'melt away,' in terror.

smoke: the smoke of villages, sacked and set on fire, heralds
the approach of the invader.

none...times: marg. 'there is no straggler in his ranks';
cf. *v.* 27.

That the LORD hath founded Zion, and in her shall the
afflicted of his people take refuge.

xv., xvi.   Oracle on Moab.

15   The burden of Moab.

---

32. The answer to the Philistine envoys. Yahwe's people
has a sure refuge in Zion, and places no reliance on arms or
alliances.

IV. Ch. xv., xvi.

The passage consists of an elegy, xv. 1–xvi. 12, on a terrible
disaster that had befallen, or was about to befall, Moab: and an
epilogue, xvi. 13, 14, which states that the preceding poem is of
earlier date, and threatens Moab with speedy and almost complete destruction.

It is improbable that both poem and epilogue are by the same
hand, and a comparison of the former with genuine writings of
Isaiah leads to the opinion that he was not its author. On the
other hand there is no convincing argument against Isaiah's
authorship of the epilogue, and the view of most scholars that
Isaiah quoted or adapted xv. 1–xvi. 12 from an earlier prophet,
and himself added xvi. 13, 14, may therefore, in the absence of
a more plausible theory, be accepted.

The poem, which appears in an expanded form in Jer. xlviii.,
may be predictive, but is more probably a vivid description of a
contemporary event. The Moabites, having suffered a crushing
blow at the hands of an invader, flee southwards to Edom
(ch. xv.), whence they send gifts to Jerusalem with a prayer for
protection (xvi. 1–5). Their request is not granted (v. 6), and
they are left without hope of succour (vv. 7–12). The historical
circumstances referred to cannot be determined with certainty.
The most plausible supposition is that the invaders were North
Israelites under Jeroboam II., who wrested back disputed
territory from both Syria and Moab (2 Kings xiv. 25, Hamath…
Arabah). His contemporary on the throne of Judah was
Uzziah, a powerful king, to whom the Moabites might naturally
look for help, especially after their flight to Edom, which was at
that time under his suzerainty. Judah, however, though
jealous of North Israel, was apparently not unwilling to see the
pride of Moab humbled, and the refusal of aid (xvi. 6) is
couched in the coldest terms. This mood is only partially shared
by the author of the poem, who appears to feel for Moab in her
calamity. Jer. xlviii., on the other hand, is strongly hostile to
Moab.

For Isaiah's addendum the most probable date is c. 711 B.C.,

For in a night Ar of Moab is laid waste, *and* brought
to nought; for in a night Kir of Moab is laid waste, *and*
brought to nought. He is gone up to Bayith, and to 2
Dibon, to the high places, to weep: Moab howleth over
Nebo, and over Medeba: on all their heads is baldness,
every beard is cut off. In their streets they gird them- 3
selves with sackcloth: on their housetops, and in their
broad places, every one howleth, weeping abundantly.
And Heshbon crieth out, and Elealeh; their voice is 4
heard even unto Jahaz: therefore the armed men of Moab
cry aloud; his soul trembleth within him. My heart 5
crieth out for Moab; her nobles *flee* unto Zoar, to Eglath-
shelishiyah: for by the ascent of Luhith with weeping

---

as the Moabites were then in revolt against Sargon, whereas at
the time of Sennacherib's campaign in 701 they remained faithful
to their Assyrian allegiance.

xv. 1. Ar of Moab (cf. Num. xxi. 15, 28) lay on the south
bank of the Arnon, probably nearly opposite Aroer. In later
times it was wrongly identified with Rabba (Areopolis), some
10 miles further south.

Kir of Moab: the modern Kerak, on the Wady Kerak, south
of Rabba, probably identical also with Kir-hareseth (xvi. 7),
and Kir-heres (xvi. 11).

These were the principal Moabite strongholds. Their loss
meant complete disaster.

2–4. Lamentation over the fall of the great strongholds
passes like a wave northwards over the region north of the
Arnon. The towns mentioned lie in this region, which was
claimed by North Israel, and was in its possession in the reigns
of Omri and Ahab, but was regained for Moab by Mesha,
probably at the close of Ahab's reign, as described on the
Moabite Stone.

2. He...places: read 'the daughter of Dibon (Bath-Dibon,
cf. Jer. xlviii. 18) is gone up to the high places.'

over...Medeba: render 'on Nebo, and on Medeba,' high-
lying towns east of the northern extremity of the Dead Sea.

5–9. Southward flight of the Moabites.

5. nobles: marg. 'fugitives.'

Zoar: not precisely identified, but probably near the S.E.
extremity of the Dead Sea.

Eglath-shelishiyah: i.e. the third Eglath, presumably one
of three villages bearing the same name.

they go up; for in the way of Horonaim they raise up a
6 cry of destruction.   For the waters of Nimrim shall be
desolate: for the grass is withered away, the tender grass
7 faileth, there is no green thing.   Therefore the abundance
they have gotten, and that which they have laid up, shall
8 they carry away to the brook of the willows.   For the cry
is gone round about the borders of Moab; the howling
thereof unto Eglaim, and the howling thereof unto Beer-
9 elim.   For the waters of Dimon are full of blood: for I will
bring yet more upon Dimon, a lion upon him that
escapeth of Moab, and upon the remnant of the land.

16   Send ye the lambs for the ruler of the land from Sela
which is toward the wilderness, unto the mount of the
2 daughter of Zion.   For it shall be that, as wandering
birds, as a scattered nest, so shall the daughters of Moab

Luhith, Horonaim, and the **waters of Nimrim** (*v.* 6) were in
the southern region of Moab, between Kerak and Zoar, but
none of them has been certainly identified.

7. abundance...laid up: i.e. their savings and their stored
wealth.

carry...willows: read 'carry over the brook of the willows,'
flowing probably through the Wady el-Ahsa into the south of
the Dead Sea, and forming the boundary between Moab and
Edom.   The region S. of the Dead Sea was called the 'Arabah,
and it is possible that the 'brook of the willows' ('arabim) may
be identical with the brook of the 'Araba, 2 Kings xiv. 25;
Amos vi. 14.

8. Eglaim and **Beer-elim** are not identified, but were presumably border towns, the whole land lying between them.

9. Dimon has been identified by an ancient conjecture with
Dibon.   The form Dimon may contain a play upon the word
for 'blood.'

xvi. 1. Send...land. Advice is offered either by the Edomites
or by Moabite chiefs in hurried council to send tribute to the
King of Judah, the overlord of the land of Edom.

Sela: generally, but not certainly, identified with Petra, both
names meaning 'rock' or 'cliff.'

which...wilderness: omit 'which is.'   The wilderness lay
between the Edomite cliffs and Jerusalem.

2. daughters of Moab: the inhabitants, regarded collectively,
of the Moabite towns; cf. Ps. xlviii. 11.

be at the fords of Arnon. Give counsel, execute judge- 3
ment ; make thy shadow as the night in the midst of the
noonday : hide the outcasts ; bewray not the wanderer.
Let mine outcasts dwell with thee ; as for Moab, be thou 4
a covert to him from the face of the spoiler : for the
extortioner is brought to nought, spoiling ceaseth, the
oppressors are consumed out of the land. And a throne 5
shall be established in mercy, and one shall sit thereon in
truth, in the tent of David ; judging, and seeking judgement, and swift to do righteousness.

We have heard of the pride of Moab, *that* he is very 6
proud ; even of his arrogancy, and his pride, and his
wrath ; his boastings are nought. Therefore shall Moab 7
howl for Moab, every one shall howl : for the raisin-cakes
of Kir-hareseth shall ye mourn, utterly stricken. For the 8
fields of Heshbon languish, *and* the vine of Sibmah ; the
lords of the nations have broken down the choice plants

3–5. The appeal of the envoys to Judah.

3. **shadow** : the symbol of protection from the fierce heat of
mid-day ; cf. xxv. 4, xxxii. 2.

4. **Let...Moab** : read 'let the outcasts of Moab sojourn with
thee' (under thy protection). Or regard 'Moab' as an explanatory
gloss : 'let my outcasts (i.e. Moab's) sojourn....'

4*b***, 5.** The text, as translated, is unintelligible in the mouth
of the Moabites, and the introduction of any other speaker is
intolerably awkward. The rendering 'when the extortioner
shall have ceased...land, then a throne...righteousness' implies
that the throne of David is to be set up in Moab. Such an offer
of unconditional subjection is not impossible ; but read preferably
'until the extortioner...land' ; and regard *v.* 5 as a fulsome
compliment on the part of the suppliants.

6. Judah remembers the haughty arrogance of Moab in the
days of his prosperity, and distrusts his present flatteries and
professions of meekness.

boastings : 'idle talk,' referring to the adulatory language of
vv. 3–5.

7. The appeal having failed, the lamentation is resumed.

raisin-cakes : cakes of compressed grapes, a favourite delicacy
at religious festivals ; cf. Hos. iii. 1 ; 2 Sam. vi. 19.

Kir-hareseth : see on xv. 1.

8. **the lords...thereof** : transl. ' whose choice clusters struck

thereof; they reached even unto Jazer, they wandered
into the wilderness; her branches were spread abroad,
9 they passed over the sea. Therefore I will weep with
the weeping of Jazer for the vine of Sibmah: I will
water thee with my tears, O Heshbon, and Elealeh: for
upon thy summer fruits and upon thy harvest the *battle*
10 shout is fallen. And gladness is taken away, and joy out
of the fruitful field; and in the vineyards there shall be
no singing, neither joyful noise: no treader shall tread out
wine in the presses; I have made the *vintage* shout to
11 cease. Wherefore my bowels sound like an harp for Moab,
12 and mine inward parts for Kir-heres. And it shall come
to pass, when Moab presenteth himself, when he wearieth
himself upon the high place, and shall come to his
sanctuary to pray, that he shall not prevail.

13 This is the word that the LORD spake concerning Moab
14 in time past. But now the LORD hath spoken, saying,
Within three years, as the years of an hireling, and the
glory of Moab shall be brought into contempt, with all

---

down (i.e. intoxicated) the lords of the nations.' The potent
wine of Sibmah was drunk to excess at the banquets of princes.

they reached...sea. The luxuriant vines are represented hyper-
bolically as extending northwards to Jazer, trailing eastwards to
the desert, and southwards as far as the Dead Sea (read ' to the
sea ').

9–11. The poet's sympathy.

9. battle shout ‖ vintage shout (*v.* 10): the same word in
the double sense of the battle-cry of troops at the charge
(cf. Jer. li. 14), and the glad shout of the grape-treaders
(Jer. xxv. 30).

10. I have...cease: read ' the vintage-shout is stilled.'

11. bowels: the seat of the most poignant emotions of
sympathy and distress; cf. Jer. iv. 9; Cant. v. 4 marg.

Kir-heres: see on xv. 1.

12. The assiduous prayers of Moab, addressed of course to
his own god Chemosh, will not avail to procure deliverance.
Cf. Jer. xlviii. 13.

13, 14. The epilogue. Moab has recovered strength since
the catastrophe, but doom is at hand.

14. as...hireling: the meaning is either that three years

his great multitude; and the remnant shall be very small
and of no account.

xvii. 1-11.   *An oracle on Damascus and Ephraim.*

The burden of Damascus.   **17**

Behold, Damascus is taken away from being a city,
and it shall be a ruinous heap. The cities of Aroer are 2
forsaken: they shall be for flocks, which shall lie down,
and none shall make them afraid.   The fortress also shall 3
cease from Ephraim, and the kingdom from Damascus,
and the remnant of Syria; they shall be as the glory of
the children of Israel, saith the LORD of hosts.

---

were a customary period for which a man hired himself (but
cf. xxi. 16); or, more probably, that the respite would not be
prolonged any more than a hireling would work for more than
the stipulated period of service.

V. Ch. xvii. 1-11.

This is one of Isaiah's early prophecies. Syria and North
Israel are in alliance, but there is no hint of a joint attack on
Judah.   The passage should therefore be dated B.C. 736 or 735,
before ch. vii., which refers to the campaign of the allies against
Judah, but possibly after ix. 8–x. 4, in which there is not yet any
indication of the Syro-Ephraimitish alliance.

The oracle is directed mainly against Ephraim, the editorial
title and the position of the piece among the oracles on foreign
nations being due to the short introductory threat against
Damascus, *vv.* 1–3.

1-3.   The ruin of Damascus.

2.   The cities of Aroer: i.e., perhaps, the villages round about
Aroer.   Neither the Aroer in Moab (Jos. xiii. 16) nor the
Aroer in Ammon (Jos. xiii. 25) can be meant here.   Nor is it
likely that any otherwise unknown village in the Syrian kingdom is referred to.   Read (on basis of LXX) 'her cities
(i.e. the daughter-cities of Damascus) are forsaken for ever.'

3.   fortress: possibly the city of Samaria, or perhaps the
strong places of Ephraim regarded collectively; but the reference is probably to Syria, which was at that time the fortress or
bulwark of Ephraim against Assyrian invasion.

and the remnant...Israel: read 'and the remnant of Syria
shall be as the glory of Israel,' i.e. shall sink as low as Israel.

4   And it shall come to pass in that day, that the glory of
Jacob shall be made thin, and the fatness of his flesh
5   shall wax lean.   And it shall be as when the harvestman
gathereth the standing corn, and his arm reapeth the
ears; yea, it shall be as when one gleaneth ears in the
6   valley of Rephaim.   Yet there shall be left therein
gleanings, as the shaking of an olive tree, two or three
berries in the top of the uppermost bough, four or five in
the outmost branches of a fruitful tree, saith the LORD,
7   the God of Israel.   In that day shall a man look unto
his Maker, and his eyes shall have respect to the
8   Holy One of Israel.   And he shall not look to the altars,
the work of his hands, neither shall he have respect to
that which his fingers have made, either the Asherim, or
9   the sun-images.   In that day shall his strong cities be as
the forsaken places in the wood and on the mountain top,

4–6. The destruction of Israel.

5. The reaper takes the ears of corn in one hand, and with
the other cuts the stalks close to the head. The remnant of
Israel will be a mere handful, like the ears of corn left for the
gleaner (cf. Ruth ii. 2, 7, 15 f.).

valley of Rephaim: a fertile plain, south of Jerusalem towards
Bethlehem, in which Isaiah and his hearers had doubtless often
seen the harvesters and gleaners.

6. shaking: marg. 'beating.' The olive tree was beaten
with a stick to bring down the fruit. A stray olive or two
might remain on the tree.

8. altars…Asherim…sun-images. These words, which
disturb the rhythm, are glosses on 'the work…hands' and
'that which…made.' The Asherim (sing. Asherah) were
sacred poles set up near an altar (cf. Deut. xvi. 21). Their
origin and significance are alike doubtful. They may have
been at first intended simply to mark the spot as sacred, or
they may have been artificial relics of the ancient tree-worship,
though they certainly became the objects of idolatrous worship
(Jud. iii. 7; 2 Kings xxiii. 4), and a goddess *Ashrat* seems to
have been worshipped in Palestine. The 'sun-images' (ham-
manim) were pillars (see on xix. 19) specially associated with
the worship of Baal-Ḥamman, the sun-god.

9–11. The continuation of *vv.* 4–6. The desolation of Israel.

9. in the…top: read, on basis of LXX, 'of the Hivites and
the Amorites.' Cf. marg.

which were forsaken from before the children of Israel:
and it shall be a desolation. For thou hast forgotten the 10
God of thy salvation, and hast not been mindful of the
rock of thy strength; therefore thou plantest pleasant
plants, and settest it with strange slips: in the day of thy 11
planting thou hedgest it in, and in the morning thou
makest thy seed to blossom: but the harvest fleeth away
in the day of grief and of desperate sorrow.

12–14. *The destruction of the Assyrian army.*

Ah, the uproar of many peoples, which roar like the 12
roaring of the seas; and the rushing of nations, that
rush like the rushing of mighty waters! The nations 13
shall rush like the rushing of many waters: but he shall

---

which were forsaken: transl. 'which they (the Hivites and
Amorites) forsook.'
10. pleasant plants: marg. 'plantings of Adonis' (Hebr.
na'ămānîm), the reference being to the cult of the Syrian god
Na'man = Adonis. The 'plantings' were the 'Adonis-gardens'
of the Greeks (Plato, *Phaedrus*, 276), pots of quickly flowering
and as quickly withering plants, which were placed at the doors
of houses or in the courts of temples. These Adonis-plants, to
the Greeks the type of short-lived pleasures, symbolise here the
short-sighted political schemes and religious innovations of Israel
under the influence of the Syrian alliance.
strange slips: either foreign vine-branches, a metaphor for
foreign customs generally, or vine-branches of a foreign god,
i.e. Adonis.
11. The foreign alliance promises to bear the fruit of immediate political success. But the plant will wither ere it
flowers, and Israel's abandonment of Yahwe will bring about
her utter desolation.

VI. Ch. xvii. 12–14.

A word of encouragement to Judah, and a threat of annihilation against the Assyrians, at or near the time of Sennacherib's
invasion (701 B.C.).
12. many peoples: the numerous subject peoples which
furnished contingents to the Assyrian army.
13, 14. At the rebuke of Yahwe the invading host is scattered.
In the evening it fills Jerusalem with terror, and by morning it
has vanished.

rebuke them, and they shall flee far off, and shall be
chased as the chaff of the mountains before the wind,
14 and like the whirling dust before the storm. At eventide
behold terror; *and* before the morning they are not.
This is the portion of them that spoil us, and the lot
of them that rob us.

xviii. *Isaiah's confident answer to the Ethiopian ambassadors.*

18 Ah, the land of the rustling of wings, which is beyond
2 the rivers of Ethiopia: that sendeth ambassadors by the
sea, even in vessels of papyrus upon the waters, *saying*,
Go, ye swift messengers, to a nation tall and smooth, to a
people terrible from their beginning onward; a nation

VII. Ch. xviii.

This passage is of about the same date as xvii. 12-14, with
which it is possibly connected. In view of the approaching
Assyrian invasion envoys from the Ethiopian king then ruling
Egypt come to Jerusalem with the object of contracting an
alliance with Hezekiah. Isaiah advises a firm refusal of their
advances on the ground that Judah is secure under the protection
of Yahwe, who will Himself destroy the Assyrian power. Cf. the
answer to the Philistine envoys in xiv. 29-32.

1. rustling of wings: an allusion to the swarms of insects
characteristic of the Upper Nile, and especially, perhaps, to the
Tsetse-fly. Cf. vii. 18.

beyond...Ethiopia. The description is vague, and the word
'beyond' cannot be pressed. The ancient Kush, or Ethiopia,
corresponded roughly to the modern Nubia, and stretched down
into the Soudan. The capital of the Ethiopian Empire in
Isaiah's time was Napata, on the westward bank of the Nile
about 18° N. The rivers meant are probably the Nile itself, the
Atbara, and the Blue Nile.

2. sea: i.e. the Nile, as in xix. 5; Nah. iii. 8. The Arabic
name for the Nile is *el-bahr* (the sea), and similar language is
used by both Greek and Latin writers.

saying, Go: omit 'saying.' Isaiah is the speaker, and
charges the envoys to return to their own land.

smooth: lit. 'polished,' a reference to the shining bronze-like
complexion of the Ethiopians, whom Herodotus (iii. 20) calls
the tallest and handsomest of men.

terrible...onward: a phrase grammatically awkward, and of

that meteth out and treadeth down, whose land the rivers
divide! All ye inhabitants of the world, and ye dwellers 3
on the earth, when an ensign is lifted up on the mountains,
see ye; and when the trumpet is blown, hear ye. For 4
thus hath the LORD said unto me, I will be still, and I
will behold in my dwelling place; like clear heat in sun-
shine, like a cloud of dew in the heat of harvest. For 5
afore the harvest, when the blossom is over, and the
flower becometh a ripening grape, he shall cut off the
sprigs with pruning-hooks, and the spreading branches
shall he take away *and* cut down. They shall be left 6
together unto the ravenous birds of the mountains, and
to the beasts of the earth: and the ravenous birds shall
summer upon them, and all the beasts of the earth shall
winter upon them. In that time shall a present be 7
brought unto the LORD of hosts of a people tall and
smooth, and from a people terrible from their beginning

---

doubtful meaning: possibly, 'dreaded from where it is (its own
land) and onwards,' i.e. 'dreaded near and far.'

a nation...down: better 'a nation strong and conquering.'

3. The answer to the envoys concerns all the peoples of the
earth, for all will be impressed by the decisive interposition of
Yahwe when the contending hosts are marshalled for the
conflict.

4. Yahwe has revealed His purpose to the prophet, who in
turn communicates it to the Ethiopian ambassadors and to the
world. Like the still, intense heat of a summer day, or the
high, white dew-cloud on a summer night, Yahwe is undisturbed
and unmoved by the ambitious schemes of conquest which seem
to be approaching fruition.

5. Favoured by the clear heat of midday, and the soft dew of
evening (*v.* 4), the grapes are ripening fast, when suddenly, at
the critical moment, the limit of Yahwe's patience is reached,
and the spreading vine-branches are ruthlessly cut down.

6. The interpretation of the metaphor in *v.* 5. For a whole
year the stricken army provides carrion for the vulture and the
beast of prey. Cf. Ezek. xxxix. 17 ff.

7. The Ethiopians will recognize the pre-eminence of Zion,
the seat of Yahwe, to whose intervention they owe their deliverance from the dread of Assyria.

of a people: read 'from a people,' as in the following clause.

onward; a nation that meteth out and treadeth down, whose land the rivers divide, to the place of the name of the LORD of hosts, the mount Zion.

xix. 1–15. An oracle on Egypt.
1–4. Anarchy and tyranny.

19   The burden of Egypt.

Behold, the LORD rideth upon a swift cloud, and cometh unto Egypt: and the idols of Egypt shall be moved at his presence, and the heart of Egypt shall melt in the
2 midst of it.   And I will stir up the Egyptians against the Egyptians: and they shall fight every one against his brother, and every one against his neighbour; city against
3 city, *and* kingdom against kingdom.   And the spirit of Egypt shall be made void in the midst of it; and I will

---

VIII. Ch. xix.

This chapter has two main sections: (1) *vv.* 1–15, which describe the overwhelming effects of Yahwe's judgment on Egypt; and (2) *vv.* 16–25, a series of brief prophecies, each introduced by the formula 'in that day.'

1–15. Under the chastising hand of Yahwe Egypt suffers from anarchy and tyrannical oppression. Physical calamities afflict the land, and industry languishes. The wisdom of the ruling classes fails, and the people are helpless.

The historical allusions in this passage are vague, and it cannot be shown that all the features of the distress here portrayed were visible in Egypt at any one time. If the passage be Isaiah's it is natural to suppose that by the 'hard lord' (*v.* 4) an Assyrian conqueror is meant, possibly Sargon or Sennacherib, though the conquest of Egypt by Assyria did not actually take place till 672 under Esar-haddon. On the other hand considerations both of style and contents lead many recent critics to refer the passage to post-exilic times, in which case the 'hard lord' may be Cambyses or Xerxes.

1. rideth...cloud: cf. Ps. civ. 3.   The thunder-cloud, symbolized by the Cherubim (cf. Ps. xviii. 10), was the emblem of Yahwe's presence.

3. made void: rather 'poured out.'

destroy the counsel thereof: and they shall seek unto the
idols, and to the charmers, and to them that have familiar
spirits, and to the wizards. And I will give over the 4
Egyptians into the hand of a cruel lord; and a fierce king
shall rule over them, saith the Lord, the LORD of hosts.

5-10. *Physical and industrial calamities.*

And the waters shall fail from the sea, and the river shall 5
be wasted and become dry. And the rivers shall stink; 6
the streams of Egypt shall be minished and dried up:
the reeds and flags shall wither away. The meadows 7
by the Nile, by the brink of the Nile, and all that is sown
by the Nile, shall become dry, be driven away, and be no
more. The fishers also shall lament, and all they that 8
cast angle into the Nile shall mourn, and they that spread
nets upon the waters shall languish. Moreover they that 9

---

destroy: better 'confuse,' as in iii. 12.

charmers: lit. 'mutterers' (of magical spells: LXX 'ven-
triloquists'). See also viii. 19.

4. Egypt will suffer cruelly under a tyrannical yoke, either
Assyrian or Persian, according to the date to which the passage
is assigned.

5-10. The calamities here described are not the result of bad
government and neglect of irrigation, but the direct consequences of Yahwe's punitive intervention.

5. sea: see on xviii. 2.

6. rivers: the canals which from early times have supplied
the soil of Egypt with water.

streams of Egypt: lit. 'the Niles,' the arms of the Nile
forming the Delta.

7. The meadows...brink of the Nile. Comparison with LXX
shows that the text is uncertain. The 'meadows' (lit. 'bare
places') may be places bare of trees, but the meaning is quite
doubtful. For **brink** read perhaps 'mouth.'

all...Nile: another doubtful expression; perhaps 'all the
seed-land of the Nile,' in which case the expression 'driven
away' is awkward. The general sense of the verse is plain,
but the exact meaning of its unusual words is a matter of
conjecture.

8. The first effect of the water famine is the destruction of
the fishing industry.

9. The ruin of the textile industry. Linen and cotton were

work in combed flax, and they that weave white cloth,
10 shall be ashamed. And her pillars shall be broken in
pieces, all they that work for hire *shall be* grieved in soul.

11–15. *The bankruptcy of Egyptian statesmanship.*

11 The princes of Zoan are utterly foolish ; the counsel of
the wisest counsellors of Pharaoh is become brutish : how
say ye unto Pharaoh, I am the son of the wise, the son of
12 ancient kings ? Where then are thy wise men ? and let
them tell thee now ; and let them know what the LORD of
13 hosts hath purposed concerning Egypt. The princes of
Zoan are become fools, the princes of Noph are deceived ;
they have caused Egypt to go astray, that are·the corner
14 stone of her tribes. The LORD hath mingled a spirit of
perverseness in the midst of her : and they have caused
Egypt to go astray in every work thereof, as a drunken
15 man staggereth in his vomit. Neither shall there be tor

---

staple manufactures of ancient Egypt. The text and the precise
meaning are doubtful.
    10. pillars: either the leading men of the country, or the
'foundations' of society, i.e. the mass of workers. The text is
obscure, and possibly 'the weavers of it' (i.e. of linen) should be
read.
    11. Zoan : Tanis, on the right bank of the Tanitic, or second
arm (the second from the east) of the Nile, the seat of the 21st
and 23rd dynasties.
    utterly foolish: rather 'mere fools,' nought but fools.
    the counsel...brutish : lit. 'the wisest counsellors of Pharaoh
are stupid counsel,' the abstract being used for the concrete.
    how say...kings: a scornful allusion to the pride of the
hereditary sacerdotal caste, the descendants of the ancient royal
houses.
    12. In the same scornful strain the prophet now addresses
Pharaoh himself.
    13. Noph : Memphis (hieroglyphic *Mennofer*) just south of
the apex of the Delta, near Cairo. In Hos. ix. 6 the same city
is called Moph.
    the corner stone of her tribes : the ruling caste, the governors
of the nomes or districts (cf. *v.* 2 'kingdoms') into which Egypt
was divided.
    14. staggereth : rather 'goeth astray,' as in the preceding
clause. For the image cf. xxviii. 7, 8.

Egypt any work, which head or tail, palm-branch or rush,
may do.

16–25. *Brief prophecies on Egypt.*

16–18. *The fear of Yahwe in Egypt.*

In that day shall Egypt be like unto women : and it 16
shall tremble and fear because of the shaking of the hand
of the LORD of hosts, which he shaketh over it. And the 17
land of Judah shall become a terror unto Egypt, every
one to whom mention is made thereof shall be afraid,
because of the purpose of the LORD of hosts, which he
purposeth against it.

In that day there shall be five cities in the land of 18
Egypt that speak the language of Canaan, and swear to

---

15. There is no cohesion among the various castes and no
united action is possible.

head...rush : see ix. 14.

16–25. This passage is probably of somewhat later date than
vv. 1–15. Its tone is much more sympathetic towards Egypt, which
is represented as submitting to Yahwe and embracing the true
faith under the influence of Jewish colonies. Hebrew is still to
be the language of these colonies (*v.* 18), which points to a time
anterior to the universal adoption of Greek as the language of
the Diaspora. The mention in *vv.* 19–22 of the erection of an
altar and pillar in Egypt, and of the offering of sacrifices there,
seems at first sight to indicate that these verses at least were
written before the publication of the Deuteronomic code; but
the whole point of the passage is that the narrow Palestinian
Judaism is to give place to a widely diffused worship of Yahwe,
and no safe inference can be drawn from these verses as to the
date of the passage, which, whether it be a unity or a collection
of detached pieces, is probably to be ascribed to the earlier days
of the Greek period.

16, 17. These verses form the connecting link between the
threats of the preceding section and the promises which follow.
The Egyptians will recognize the hand of Yahwe in their
calamities, and will be filled with dread of Him and of the land
of Judah, which is in a special sense His land. This may be
regarded as the first step in their conversion.

18. The five cities contain colonies of Hebrew-speaking
Jews, and become centres from which the knowledge of Yahwe
may be diffused over the whole land.

the LORD of hosts; one shall be called The city of destruction.

19-22. Altar and sacrifice in Egypt.

19 In that day shall there be an altar to the LORD in the midst of the land of Egypt, and a pillar at the border
20 thereof to the LORD.   And it shall be for a sign and for a witness unto the LORD of hosts in the land of Egypt: for they shall cry unto the LORD because of the oppressors, and he shall send them a saviour, and a defender, and he

---

city of destruction. There are three variants of the mysterious name of this city: (1) 'city of destruction,' an obscure reading which can hardly mean 'city of the destruction of idols,' but must be taken in a sense hostile to the city, whereas the general tone of the passage is sympathetic to the Jewish colonies. The rendering of the same reading 'city of the lion' (= Leontopolis) is based on a dubious Arabic analogy. (2) 'city of the sun' (= Heliopolis); cf. Jer. xliii. 13 marg. The difference in Hebrew between this reading and (1) is extremely slight, and they might easily be confused.   The Jewish temple in Egypt was built about 160 B.C. in Leontopolis, in the district of Heliopolis. The temple was founded by Onias, the legitimate heir to the high-priesthood, who, owing to party conflicts, was a fugitive from Jerusalem, and had placed himself under the protection of Ptolemy Philometor. (3) The LXX translators, naturally favourable to the Egyptian temple, read 'city of righteousness.'   It is clear that the variants represent two views of the temple at Leontopolis, one friendly and the other hostile.   But the original reading is doubtful.   It may have been 'city of the sun,' in definite reference to Heliopolis, while the other variants represent respectively the Palestinian and Egyptian attitudes to the temple of Onias.

19. The pillar at the border of Egypt was to be a visible token that Yahwe was worshipped in the land, which was therefore under His protection. It is not necessary to suppose that such a pillar was an object of worship.

According to Josephus Onias appealed to this verse in justification of his action in founding the temple at Leontopolis.

20. In any time of calamity and oppression the care of Yahwe will provide deliverance and defence for His new people. The language is indefinite, and there does not appear to be any special historical allusion in the verse.

shall deliver them. And the LORD shall be known to 21
Egypt, and the Egyptians shall know the LORD in that
day; yea, they shall worship with sacrifice and oblation,
and shall vow a vow unto the LORD, and shall perform it.
And the LORD shall smite Egypt, smiting and healing; 22
and they shall return unto the LORD, and he shall be
intreated of them, and shall heal them.

23-25. *The triple alliance of the Messianic age.*

In that day shall there be a high way out of Egypt to 23
Assyria, and the Assyrian shall come into Egypt, and the
Egyptian into Assyria; and the Egyptians shall worship
with the Assyrians.

In that day shall Israel be the third with Egypt and 24
with Assyria, a blessing in the midst of the earth: for 25
that the LORD of hosts hath blessed them, saying, Blessed
be Egypt my people, and Assyria the work of my hands,
and Israel mine inheritance.

---

21. Experience of Yahwe's protecting care will extend the
knowledge of Him in Egypt, and will intensify the Egyptians'
gratitude, and their desire to worship and obey Him.

22. Further chastisements of Egypt will be the chastisements
of discipline. Yahwe will smite in order to heal.

23. A highway of peaceful intercourse will join Egypt and
Assyria (=Syria, as in xi. 11), passing through Palestine, and
Syria also will join Egypt in the worship of Yahwe.

24, 25. The three kingdoms of Egypt, Syria, and Israel,
politically equal and independent, will be united by a common
faith, and of this league Israel will be the religious as well as
the geographical centre.

25. Israel is no longer the sole people of Yahwe, but it
retains a position of pre-eminence as in a special sense His
inheritance.

xx. *A prediction of the Assyrian conquest of Egypt and Ethiopia.*

20 In the year that Tartan came unto Ashdod, when Sargon the king of Assyria sent him, and he fought 2 against Ashdod and took it; at that time the LORD spake by Isaiah the son of Amoz, saying, Go, and loose the sackcloth from off thy loins, and put thy shoe from off thy 3 foot. And he did so, walking naked and barefoot. And the LORD said, Like as my servant Isaiah hath walked naked and barefoot three years for a sign and a wonder 4 upon Egypt and upon Ethiopia; so shall the king of Assyria lead away the captives of Egypt, and the exiles of Ethiopia, young and old, naked and barefoot, and with 5 buttocks uncovered, to the shame of Egypt. And they shall be dismayed and ashamed, because of Ethiopia 6 their expectation, and of Egypt their glory. And the

---

IX. Ch. xx.

The king of Ashdod attempted to form a confederacy of Palestinian and neighbouring states to resist the Assyrian rule, relying on the help of Egypt. The attempt was crushed by the capture and sack of Ashdod in 711 B.C., which is therefore the date of this prophecy. As a symbolic warning of the futility of all hope of effective assistance from Egypt, Isaiah went about in the garb of a beggar or captive for the three years preceding 711, this being a type of the straits to which Egypt would soon be reduced.

1. Tartan: the official title of the Assyrian commander-in-chief.

Sargon. This king, of whom this is the only mention in O.T., reigned from 722 to 705 B.C.

2. An explanatory parenthesis.

at that time. The expression is vague, the actual time being three years before the present prophecy.

sackcloth...naked. Isaiah put off his outer garment of coarse hairy material, and retained only the under garment. Thus insufficiently clad, he is described as naked.

5. they: i.e. those in Philistia and Judah who had hoped for Ethiopian intervention in their behalf, and had boasted of the power of Egypt.

inhabitant of this coastland shall say in that day, Behold,
such is our expectation, whither we fled for help to be
delivered from the king of Assyria : and we, how shall we
escape?

xxi. *Oracles on Babylon, Edom, and Dedan.*

1-10. *The fall of Babylon.*

The burden of the wilderness of the sea.　　　　**21**

As whirlwinds in the South sweep through, it cometh
from the wilderness, from a terrible land. A grievous 2
vision is declared unto me ; the treacherous dealer dealeth
treacherously, and the spoiler spoileth. Go up, O Elam ;
besiege, O Media ; all the sighing thereof have I made to
cease. Therefore are my loins filled with anguish ; pangs 3

---

6. coastland: strictly Philistia, but here obviously including
Judah, which Isaiah specially desired to warn against illusory
hopes of Egyptian aid.

X. Ch. xxi.

These oracles closely resemble one another alike in their compressed and obscure style and in the spirit in which they
describe disasters to the enemies of Israel. There is no jubila-
tion in them but rather a sense of awe in the contemplation of
great calamities, and a shuddering dread of the horrors of war.
They are probably to be ascribed to the same author, and
should be dated 549-538 B.C., the first oracle clearly referring to
the imminent attack on Babylon by Cyrus.

1. burden...sea. The editorial title of the oracle 'wilderness
of the sea,' or, with LXX, simply 'wilderness,' seems to be
suggested by the prominent occurrence of the word in *v.* 1.

South : the Negeb, properly the region just south of Judah,
but used also as a geographical term meaning 'south.'

it...land. The vague terrible danger approaches from the
wilderness, probably the plain between Babylonia and Elam,
which is itself the 'terrible land.'

2. grievous vision. The vision is 'hard,' as portending
grim war and bloodshed.

the treacherous...cease. The simplest interpretation of
these obscure clauses is to take the whole as the words of
Yahwe addressed to Cyrus, containing (*a*) a complaint of the
treachery and cruelty of Babylon, (*b*) the command to proceed
to the attack, (*c*) a promise of victory, which will bring to an
end the sighing caused by Babylonian oppression.

have taken hold upon me, as the pangs of a woman in
travail : I am pained so that I cannot hear; I am dismayed
4 so that I cannot see. My heart panteth, horror hath
affrighted me : the twilight that I desired hath been
5 turned into trembling unto me. They prepare the table,
they set the watch, they eat, they drink : rise up, ye
6 princes, anoint the shield. For thus hath the Lord said
unto me, Go, set a watchman; let him declare what he
7 seeth : and when he seeth a troop, horsemen in pairs, a
troop of asses, a troop of camels, he shall hearken
8 diligently with much heed. And he cried as a lion: O
Lord, I stand continually upon the watch-tower in the day-
9 time, and am set in my ward whole nights: and, behold,
here cometh a troop of men, horsemen in pairs. And he

3, 4. The effect of this vision and spiritual audition of the
voice of Yahwe proclaiming the doom of Babylon is to fill the
prophet with terror and anxiety. Even the pleasant hour of
meditation in the cool of sunset loses its charm, perhaps
because it was then that he saw the 'hard vision.'

Note the absence of any burning hatred of Babylon or fierce
joy at its downfall. The prophet is perturbed by the anticipa-
tion of the horrors which might be expected to accompany the
siege and sack of the city.

5. In striking contrast to the prophet's anxiety the Babylonian nobles feast at ease until awakened to a sense of their
danger by the sudden call to arms.

set the watch : marg. 'spread the carpets.'

6-9. The details of the 'hard vision.'

6. watchman. The prophet dissociates from his own personality that part of himself which is susceptible to Divine
communication. This spiritually receptive element in his own
consciousness he calls the watchman, who sees, and declares
what he sees.

7. The vision of a military train of horses, asses, and camels
is to warn the watchman that the voice of Yahwe may now be
heard.

8. as a lion. The text is corrupt. Read perhaps 'I see,'
the beginning of the watchman's speech.

9. The watchman declares that he has seen the appointed
vision, and proceeds immediately to announce the significance of
what he has seen and heard. The fall of Babylon is at hand.
In the purpose of God, now revealed, the city is fallen already.

answered and said, Babylon is fallen, is fallen; and all
the graven images of her gods are broken unto the
ground. O thou my threshing, and the corn of my floor: 10
that which I have heard from the LORD of hosts, the God
of Israel, have I declared unto you.

11, 12. *Oracle on Edom.*

The burden of Dumah.   11

One calleth unto me out of Seir, Watchman, what of
the night? Watchman, what of the night? The watchman 12
said, The morning cometh, and also the night: if ye will
inquire, inquire ye: turn ye, come.

13-17. *Oracle on the Dedanites.*

The burden upon Arabia.   13

---

10. corn of my floor: read 'my child of the threshing-floor'
(see marg.). The epithets describe Israel as crushed by the
threshing-flail of Babylonian oppression.

11. Dumah: i.e. 'silence,' possibly a mysterious play upon
the somewhat similar name Edom, meaning that the oracle is in
fact silent as to Edom's fate. LXX reads simply 'Edom.'

One calleth...night: from Seir (= Edom) comes the cry,
anxiously repeated, 'watchman, how far is the night spent?—
how long must we wait for the dawn?' The night presumably
typifies the anxiety caused in Edom by the campaigns of Cyrus.
The 'watchman' is here the guard, or night-patrol, and not as
in *v.* 6 one who is on the look out. But though a different word
is used it is still the prophet's spiritual consciousness that is
meant.

12. The answer is enigmatic. The dawn comes and another
night follows. Anxiety and distress will be relieved, but
perhaps only for a breathing space. Or, for one the dawn will
break, while night descends on another. The prophet leaves
the Edomites in the dark, but invites them to consult him again.

13-15. Owing to the approaching Persian invasion (see
introductory note to ch. xxi.) the caravans of Dedan will be
obliged to leave the main trade-routes, and take refuge in the
bush, where they will be in dire straits for want of food and
drink.

13. The burden upon Arabia: rather 'the oracle "in the
wilderness,"' the title being taken, as in *v.* 1, from a word
occurring early in the oracle.

In the forest in Arabia shall ye lodge, O ye travelling
14 companies of Dedanites. Unto him that was thirsty
they brought water ; the inhabitants of the land of Tema
15 did meet the fugitives with their bread. For they fled
away from the swords, from the drawn sword, and from
16 the bent bow, and from the grievousness of war. For
thus hath the Lord said unto me, Within a year, according
to the years of an hireling, and all the glory of Kedar
17 shall fail: and the residue of the number of the archers,
the mighty men of the children of Kedar, shall be few:
for the LORD, the God of Israel, hath spoken it.

xxii. 1-14. *The inexpiable sin of Jerusalem.*

22   The burden of the valley of vision.

In the...Dedanites: transl. ' in the scrub in the wilderness
shall ye pass the night, ye caravans of Dedanites.' The Dedanites, a great tribe of Arab traders, had their headquarters not
far from Edom. See Jer. xlix. 8; Ez. xxv. 13, xxvii. 15, 20,
xxxviii. 13. For 'in the wilderness' LXX reads less suitably
'in the evening' (marg.).
14. The verbs are imperatives : ' bring water, ye inhabitants
...meet the fugitive' (marg.). **Tema** was an important trading
centre between Damascus and Arabia.
16, 17. A later prose appendix pronouncing the doom of
Ḳedar, a North Arabian nomadic tribe, here apparently regarded as including the Dedanites. For the phraseology cf.
xvi. 13 f., of which these verses may be an imitation.

XI. Ch. xxii. 1-14.

On some occasion of popular rejoicing Isaiah denounces the
light-headed folly of the people, closing with the terrific warning
that such impenitence and spiritual insensibility are inexpiable,
and that no forgiveness will stay the inevitable doom.
The date of the prophecy is almost certainly 701 B.C., the
period of Sennacherib's invasion, but the precise event that
occasioned the demonstration of popular joy cannot be determined with certainty. It may have been some festival uncon-
nected with the war, or possibly the brief respite purchased by
Hezekiah's submission and payment of tribute (2 Kings xviii.
14-16). But the passage gains strikingly in both force and
interest if we take it as the prophet's rebuke to the heedlessly
jubilant populace on the occasion of the retreat of Sennacherib's

What aileth thee now, that thou art wholly gone up to the housetops? O thou that art full of shoutings, a tumultuous 2 city, a joyous town; thy slain are not slain with the sword, neither are they dead in battle. All thy rulers fled away 3 together, they were bound by the archers: all that were found of thee were bound together, they fled afar off. Therefore said I, Look away from me, I will weep bitterly; 4 labour not to comfort me, for the spoiling of the daughter of my people. For it is a day of discomfiture, and of 5 treading down, and of perplexity, from the Lord, the LORD of hosts, in the valley of vision; a breaking down of the walls, and a crying to the mountains. And Elam 6

---

plague-stricken host. Isaiah has clearly hoped that the extreme peril of the city, and its unexpected deliverance—the fulfilment of his own unheeded prediction—would be received by the people, or by many of them, as a solemn message from Yahwe, calling them to repentance and faith. Instead of this he sees nothing around him but blind materialism and insensate frivolity. The most drastic discipline, short of total destruction, has failed. The sin of the people is inexpiable, and the prophet's mind is filled with dark forebodings of another and more terrible siege, with no interposition of the Divine hand to save the city from its fate.

1. The burden...vision: 'the oracle "valley of vision,"' a title taken from *v.* 5.

What...now: rather 'what meanest thou, pray?'

housetops. The flat roofs of the houses were crowded with holiday-makers, watching the scenes in the streets below.

2 *b*, 3. The dead have not fallen with honour on the field of battle; the officers have fled, without using the bow (marg.), and have been ignominiously captured by the enemy. *V.* 2 *b* alone might mean that the dead had succumbed to disease, but along with *v.* 3 it suggests that they have been put to death as prisoners. These *vv.* may refer to the campaign of Sennacherib, but are more probably the beginning of the dark vision of future discomfiture resumed in *vv.* 5-7.

4. The vision overwhelms the prophet, and he begs those who would comfort him to desist, and leave him to his grief.

5. For it...hosts: transl. 'for a day of tumult...hath Yahwe of hosts.' See on ii. 12.

in the valley...mountains: 'in the valley of vision they batter down the walls, and there is a cry (of distress, or for help) to the mountains.' The 'valley of vision' is doubtless a ravine

bare the quiver, with chariots of men *and* horsemen; and
7 Kir uncovered the shield. And it came to pass, that thy
choicest valleys were full of chariots, and the horsemen
8 set themselves in array at the gate. And he took away
the covering of Judah; and thou didst look in that day to
9 the armour in the house of the forest. And ye saw the
breaches of the city of David, that they were many: and
10 ye gathered together the waters of the lower pool. And
ye numbered the houses of Jerusalem, and ye brake down
11 the houses to fortify the wall. Ye made also a reservoir
between the two walls for the water of the old pool: but
ye looked not unto him that had done this, neither had ye

near the walls, possibly the Tyropoeon valley, in which the prophet, in his vision, saw the besiegers pressing on the final assault.

6, 7. A fragment of a description of the invading army, possibly Sennacherib's, but more probably the visionary host of *v.* 5.

6. Elam was not yet completely subject to Assyria, but might well furnish archers to the great army. **Kir** has not been identified, but was already an Assyrian province (Amos i. 5; 2 Kings xvi. 9).

with…horsemen: better, omitting 'men,' 'with chariots and cavalry.'

uncovered the shield: made ready for action by taking their shields out of their leather cases.

8-11. A sudden transition from the vision (*v.* 7) to a description of the measures of defence hurriedly undertaken when Sennacherib's army was approaching the city.

8. And he…Judah…look: the sense is doubtful; perhaps 'and when he (the enemy) removed (in his conquering march) the bulwarks of Judah, then thou didst look….'

house of the forest. See 1 Kings v. 2; x. 17. The house was evidently used as an arsenal.

9 b-11. Recent critics regard this prosaic enumeration of defensive preparations as an interpolation, but it is not without point: 'you did every single thing you could think of—except turn to God.'

10. numbered. A census of houses was taken in order that any that were superfluous might be used to provide materials for the walls.

11. him that had…ago. Yahwe had shaped the course of

respect unto him that fashioned it long ago. And in that 12
day did the Lord, the LORD of hosts, call to weeping, and
to mourning, and to baldness, and to girding with sackcloth: and behold, joy and gladness, slaying oxen and 13
killing sheep, eating flesh and drinking wine: let us eat
and drink, for to-morrow we shall die. And the LORD of 14
hosts revealed himself in mine ears, Surely this iniquity
shall not be purged from you till ye die, saith the Lord,
the LORD of hosts.

15-25. *Invective against Shebna.*
15-18. *Shebna is denounced and threatened with exile and death.*

Thus saith the Lord, the LORD of hosts, Go, get thee 15
unto this treasurer, even unto Shebna, which is over the

---

destiny, and determined with a far-sighted purpose the ex-
periences of Judah. Yet at heart, whatever their external
observances may have been, the people simply ignored Him.

12, 14. By sudden deliverance as well as by extreme peril
Yahwe had summoned the people to humiliation and repentance.
Their careless revelry mocked alike His discipline and His
grace. Their catchword of a sensual materialism, 'to-morrow
we die,' evokes the stern and final response, 'For this sin ye
shall surely die.'

XII. Ch. xxii. 15-25.

Shebna, the king's steward, or vizier, appears from his name
to have been a foreigner. He was doubtless the leader of the
party favourable to the intrigue with Egypt which Isaiah so
resolutely denounced. The tone of this invective, however,
suggests that Isaiah detested and despised him on personal as
well as political grounds. From 2 Kings xviii. 18, 37, xix. 2
(= Is. xxxvi. 3, 22, xxxvii. 2) it appears that at the final crisis
of Sennacherib's invasion Shebna was Eliakim's subordinate.
If this statement be correct we must infer that Isaiah's denunciation was made somewhat before that date, and that
Shebna's fall was only a partial one.

15. treasurer: marg. 'steward.' The title does not occur
elsewhere in O.T.

16 house, *and say*, What doest thou here? and whom hast
thou here, that thou hast hewed thee out here a sepulchre?
hewing him out a sepulchre on high, graving an habitation
17 for himself in the rock! Behold, the LORD will hurl thee
away violently as a *strong* man; yea, he will wrap thee
18 up closely. He will surely turn and toss thee like a ball
into a large country; there shalt thou die, and there shall
be the chariots of thy glory, thou shame of thy lord's
house.

19–23. *The elevation of Eliakim.*

19 And I will thrust thee from thine office, and from thy
20 station shall he pull thee down. And it shall come to
pass in that day, that I will call my servant Eliakim the
21 son of Hilkiah: and I will clothe him with thy robe, and
strengthen him with thy girdle, and I will commit thy
government into his hand: and he shall be a father to.
the inhabitants of Jerusalem, and to the house of Judah.

---

16. The foreign adventurer roused Isaiah's indignation by his
ambition to possess a splendid tomb in Jerusalem and by his
general ostentation (*v.* 18).

whom...here: a contemptuous reference to Shebna's foreign
birth.

17, 18. The marginal readings are preferable. Yahwe will
seize Shebna with a firm grip, roll him up and hurl him into a
'wide land,' probably the Assyrian Empire. His splendid
chariots (*v.* 18) will but carry him into exile, and he will never
rest in his rock-hewn tomb.

19. This verse is pitched in a lower key than the vehement
invective which precedes it, the prophet's passion cooling as he
passes from general denunciation to a practical measure of
reform.

I...he. The subject is Yahwe in both cases. It is to be
presumed that Hezekiah had already consented to Shebna's
dismissal.

20. Eliakim: doubtless the political leader of the party
opposed to the Egyptian alliance.

21. a father: a wise counsellor of the king, and a beneficent
ruler of the people.

And the key of the house of David will I lay upon his 22
shoulder ; and he shall open, and none shall shut ; and he
shall shut, and none shall open.   And I will fasten him 23
as a nail in a sure place ; and he shall be for a throne of
glory to his father's house.

24, 25.   *The nepotism and disgrace of Eliakim's house.*

And they shall hang upon him all the glory of his father's 24
house, the offspring and the issue, every small vessel, from
the vessels of cups even to all the vessels of flagons.   In 25
that day, saith the LORD of hosts, shall the nail that was
fastened in a sure place give way ; and it shall be hewn
down, and fall, and the burden that was upon it shall be
cut off ; for the LORD hath spoken it.

xxiii.   *Oracle on Phoenicia.*

The burden of Tyre.   **23**

---

22.   key...shoulder : he will have the responsibility of un-
questioned authority. Cf. ix. 6 ; Rev. iii. 7.

23.   The metaphors of the nail firmly fixed, so that it may
bear the weight of what is hung on it, and the honourable seat,
both imply that Eliakim's accession to power will give his family
an assured place among the hereditary aristocracy.

24, 25.   It is hardly possible that Isaiah can have promised the
house of Eliakim an assured place, and in the same breath have
predicted its ruin ; and there is no indication that the disgrace
threatened in *v.* 25 is conditional upon the practice of nepotism
by Eliakim and his family.   These verses are a later appendix
added when Eliakim's house had fallen into disrepute.

24.   A contemptuous description of Eliakim's, or his successors', abuse of the patronage of lucrative appointments, one
of which is found for every offshoot of the family tree.

XIII.   Ch. xxiii.

The chapter falls into two sections : (*a*) *vv.* 1–14, a poem
describing the anticipated destruction of Tyre and Sidon, the
great commercial cities of Phoenicia ; (*b*) *vv.* 15–18, a prose
appendix predicting the partial restoration of Tyre after 70
years.

It is generally agreed that the appendix is later than the
poem, and is post-exilic.   The date of the poem is quite un-

1–14. The downfall.

Howl, ye ships of Tarshish; for it is laid waste, so that there is no house, no entering in: from the land of Kittim
2 it is revealed to them. Be still, ye inhabitants of the isle; thou whom the merchants of Zidon, that pass over
3 the sea, have replenished. And on great waters the seed of Shihor, the harvest of the Nile, was her revenue;
4 and she was the mart of nations. Be thou ashamed, O Zidon: for the sea hath spoken, the strong hold of the sea, saying, I have not travailed, nor brought forth, neither have I nourished young men, nor brought up virgins.

---

certain. If it be by Isaiah its occasion may have been the campaign of Shalmaneser IV (727–722 B.C.) against Phoenicia, or, less probably, that of Sennacherib just before the invasion of Judah in 701. Possible occasions after Isaiah's time are the campaigns of Assurbanipal (668 B.C.) and Nebuchadnezzar (586 B.C.); cf. Ez. xxvi. The language of the poem is general, and gives no precise indication of date. Sidon was ravaged by Esarhaddon in 678, but Tyre did not fall to assault till it succumbed to Alexander the Great.

The poem has three strophes, *vv.* 1–5, *vv.* 6–9, *vv.* 10–14.

1. Tarshish: see on ii. 16.

for it...them: read 'for your harbours (lit. 'house') are destroyed; as they came from Kittim (Cyprus) it was made known to them.' News of the disaster reaches the Phoenician merchantmen as they approach their own land.

2. isle: marg. 'coast' (of Phoenicia).

Zidon. In this elegy Sidon, the older though subsequently less famous of the two great Phoenician cities, appears along with Tyre, equalling her in commercial enterprise, and suffering a like disaster.

3. Shihor: the Nile, as in Jer. ii. 18.

and she...nations: rather 'and it (her revenue) was the gain of the nations.' The sense seems to be that many nations benefited by the commercial activity of the Phoenicians. The Egyptian corn-trade was of great importance, but was far from being the main source of Phoenician wealth, and it is possible that the text is corrupt.

4. the strong hold of the sea: i.e. Tyre. But the clause is a gloss. The sea itself, orphaned by the destruction of the Phoenicians, cries out in anguish.

When the report cometh to Egypt, they shall be sorely 5
pained at the report of Tyre.   Pass ye over to Tarshish ; 6
howl, ye inhabitants of the isle.   Is this your joyous *city*, 7
whose antiquity is of ancient days, whose feet carried her
afar off to sojourn?   Who hath purposed this against Tyre, 8
the crowning *city*, whose merchants are princes, whose
traffickers are the honourable of the earth?   The LORD 9
of hosts hath purposed it, to stain the pride of all glory,
to bring into contempt all the honourable of the earth.
Pass through thy land as the Nile, O daughter of Tarshish; 10
there is no girdle *about thee* any more.   He hath stretched 11
out his hand over the sea, he hath shaken the kingdoms :
the LORD hath given commandment concerning Canaan,
to destroy the strong holds thereof.   And he said, Thou 12
shalt no more rejoice, O thou oppressed virgin daughter
of Zidon : arise, pass over to Kittim ; even there shalt
thou have no rest.   Behold, the land of the Chal- 13
deans ; this people is no more ; the Assyrian hath

---

5.   Egypt has cause to fear that the fall of Tyre will open the
way for an attack on herself.

6.   Pass...Tarshish: i.e. take refuge in your distant colonies.

7.   whose feet...sojourn.   Phoenician traders had settled in
remote places like Carthage and Tartessus.

8.   the crowning city : 'the giver of crowns,' an allusion to
the vassal kings who reigned in some Phoenician colonies.

10.   The text is corrupt and yields no sense.   LXX text
bids the Phoenicians cultivate their soil, because the merchant
ships will no longer come to them.   Conjectural emendation
gives the possible sense 'Lament, ye ships of Tarshish, for your
harbours are no more.'

11.   kingdoms : more especially Phoenicia and her colonies.

Canaan : here only in O.T. restricted to Phoenicia, in accordance with the usage of the Phoenicians themselves.

12.   oppressed : rather 'ravished'; the captured city is no
longer virgin.

13.   The verse is unintelligible as it stands, and is not im-
proved by any slight alterations.   The general meaning of R.V.
translation is that the fate of the Chaldaeans (presumably when
some revolt was crushed by the Assyrians) should serve as a
warning to Tyre.   But this translation is really conjectural.

appointed it for the beasts of the wilderness: they set up
their towers, they overthrew the palaces thereof; he made
14 it a ruin.   Howl, ye ships of Tarshish: for your strong
hold is laid waste.

15-18.   *The restoration.*

15 And it shall come to pass in that day, that Tyre shall be
forgotten seventy years, according to the days of one
king: after the end of seventy years it shall be unto Tyre
16 as in the song of the harlot.   Take an harp, go about the
city, thou harlot that hast been forgotten; make sweet
melody, sing many songs, that thou mayest be remembered.
17 And it shall come to pass after the end of seventy years,
that the LORD will visit Tyre, and she shall return to her
hire, and shall play the harlot with all the kingdoms of
the world upon the face of the earth.   And her merchandise and her hire shall be holiness to the LORD: it shall
not be treasured nor laid up; for her merchandise shall

LXX takes the verse as a continuation of *v.* 12, '(pass over to
Kittim...) or to the land of the Chaldaeans, and it also has been
laid waste by the Assyrians and its wall is fallen.'   Apart from
the unsuitable 'Chaldaeans' this gives a good sense, and the
name of a possible refuge for the Phoenicians might be substituted for 'Chaldaeans,' if the historical occasion were not so
entirely uncertain.

15.   seventy years: a reminiscence of Jer. xxv. 11 f., xxix. 10.

according...king: either, as long as the probable reign of a
single king or dynasty, or, more probably, with as little change
as is to be expected in the policy of a country as long as the
same king reigns.

16.   The 'song of the harlot' (*v.* 15).   The verse, which has
a lilting rhythm, is doubtless quoted from a current popular song.
A harlot, whose day of beauty is past, is bidden sing and play in
order to regain the favour she has lost.

17, 18.   Like the forgotten harlot Tyre will resume her
commercial activity (here, as in Rev. xviii. 3, compared to
harlotry), but her gains (the word used is the technical term
for the hire of a harlot) will be dedicated to Yahwe, and used
for the benefit of the Jewish people, instead of being reserved,
as in former days, for the use of the Tyrians themselves.   The

be for them that dwell before the LORD, to eat sufficiently, and for durable clothing.

---

underlying conception is that of a temple-prostitute whose hire was dedicated to the god she served. In the case of Tyre the profits of her commerce, or 'harlotry,' are to be diverted into Jewish coffers.

Ch. xxiv.–xxvii. THE DIVINE JUDGMENT ON THE WORLD, AND THE SALVATION OF ISRAEL.

The theme of these chapters, which, as they stand, form a distinct section of the book of Isaiah, is judgment and salvation. The course of thought is as follows:—the world is desolate owing to its guilt, and God is about to bring yet further desolation upon it, and in judgment finally to destroy the guilty (xxiv.); the judgment will be followed by the establishment in perfect blessedness of the divine kingdom on earth (xxv. 6–8); Israel must shelter himself while the storm breaks on the heathen empires (xxvi. 20–xxvii. 1), after which the faithful will be gathered to Zion from the ends of the earth (xxvii. 12, 13). Alongside of this main theme, and sometimes interrupting it, are lyric passages in which the Jewish community gives expression to its faith, gratitude, and aspiration (xxv. 1–5, 9–12, xxvi. 1–19, xxvii. 2–6).

The whole passage—the question of its unity being reserved—is to be assigned to the post-exilic period. Judgment has already fallen both on Israel and his oppressors (xxvii. 7 f.), and the people have been subject to more than one foreign master (xxvi. 13). The style and imagery exhibit some striking affinities with those of the apocalyptic literature, e.g. the prominence of eschatological conceptions (xxiv. 21 f.), the vagueness of the historical references, and the veiling of the identity of places and events by the use of allusive or symbolic language (xxv. 2, xxvi. 5, xxvii. 1). The two most striking ideas of the passage, the universality of the divine kingdom and salvation (xxv. 6–8), and the hope of resurrection (xxvi. 19) and immortality (xxv. 8), while not requiring a late date, certainly support it. A more precise determination of date is impossible, owing to the absence of explicit historical references, and to the darkness which envelopes Jewish history during the greater part of the post-exilic period. Perhaps the most satisfactory date is to be found in the late Persian or Greek periods (4th or 3rd century B.C.). Conjectural identifications of the places and events vaguely referred to are of little value. (See on xxiv. 14–16, xxv. 1–5.)

xxiv. 1-3. A brief introductory prediction of the impending universal judgment.

24   Behold, the LORD maketh the earth empty, and maketh
it waste, and turneth it upside down, and scattereth
2 abroad the inhabitants thereof.   And it shall be, as with
the people, so with the priest; as with the servant, so
with his master; as with the maid, so with her mistress;
as with the buyer, so with the seller; as with the lender, so
with the borrower; as with the taker of usury, so with the
3 giver of usury to him.   The earth shall be utterly emptied,
and utterly spoiled; for the LORD hath spoken this word.

These general indications of late date are the same throughout
the chapters, and do not greatly affect the question of their
unity.   On the latter note that (1) the main thread of the
prophecy may be followed through xxiv., xxv. 6-8, xxvi. 20-
xxvii. 1, xxvii. 12, 13, which form a single connected piece:
(2) two lyric passages, xxv. 1-5, xxvii. 2-6, are obviously
unrelated to their context: (3) in these passages and in two
others, xxv. 9-12, xxvi. 1-19, the nation gives thanks for
victories already won, whereas the main prophecy describes
the existing situation as altogether gloomy; on the other hand
the prediction of the destruction of Moab (xxv. 9-12) and the
subdued tone of parts of xxvi. 1-19 (e.g. *vv.* 16-18) make it
impossible to accept the view that the lyric passages are put
by the prophet into the mouth of the redeemed community of
the future: (4) xxvii. 7-11 have resemblances to both the
prophecy and the songs, but no clear affinity with either, and
must be regarded as an obscure fragment.   Distinguish therefore
(*a*) the main prophecy, as above: (*b*) the lyrics, of a somewhat
later date: (*c*) xxvii. 7-11.

Ch. xxiv.

1.   maketh...turneth...scattereth: a description not of what
Yahwe has just done, or is doing, but of what He is on the
point of doing.
    2.   The judgment affects all ranks and classes of society.
    people...priest: the distinction is social rather than religious.
The priests represent the cultivated governing class, which in
the post-exilic Jewish community was largely a priestly caste.

4-13. *The existing dismal condition of the world—*
a presage of its coming doom.

The earth mourneth and fadeth away, the world lan- 4
guisheth and fadeth away, the lofty people of the
earth do languish.   The earth also is polluted under 5
the inhabitants thereof; because they have transgressed
the laws, changed the ordinance, broken the everlasting
covenant.   Therefore hath the curse devoured the earth, 6
and they that dwell therein are found guilty : therefore
the inhabitants of the earth are burned, and few men left.
The new wine mourneth, the vine languisheth, all the 7
merryhearted do sigh.   The mirth of tabrets ceaseth, the 8
noise of them that rejoice endeth, the joy of the harp
ceaseth.   They shall not drink wine with a song ; strong 9
drink shall be bitter to them that drink it.   The city of 10
confusion is broken down: every house is shut up, that

---

5. The earth...thereof. The idea that the holy land of Israel
was profaned by the sins of the people (Jer. iii. 1; Ps. cvi. 38) is
here extended to the whole earth.

everlasting covenant: an allusion to the covenant with
Noah (Gen. ix. 16), in which the main stress was laid on the
prohibition of murder (*ib.* 5, 6).

6. Bloodshed, in violation of the 'everlasting covenant,' is
at once the physical and moral cause of the desolation of the
world.

7-9. Music and merriment have vanished from the earth.
Singing no longer accompanies the drinking of wine, which has
now (the tenses in *v.* 9 should be present) a bitter taste.

10. city of confusion: 'the waste city' (lit. 'the city of
chaos'; cf. 'waste' or 'chaos,' Gen. i. 2).   The word may be
used collectively (so LXX 'every city'), but the natural
interpretation is that the writer refers to his own city, Jerusalem.
The idea that Babylon or some other heathen city is meant rests
partly on an unnecessary identification of this city with that
mentioned in xxv. 2, and partly on the supposition that it was
the distress of this city that called forth the expressions of joy in
vv. 14-16.   In fact, however, the prophet writes sympathetically
of this city, he is distressed at its desolation, and *vv.* 16 *b* ff.
show that he anticipated yet gloomier days before the final
judgment and deliverance.

11 no man may come in. There is a crying in the streets
because of the wine; all joy is darkened, the mirth of the
12 land is gone. In the city is left desolation, and the gate
13 is smitten with destruction. For thus shall it be in the
midst of the earth among the peoples, as the shaking of
an olive tree, as the grape gleanings when the vintage is
done.

14-16. *Echoes of premature rejoicing.*

14 These shall lift up their voice, they shall shout; for
the majesty of the LORD they cry aloud from the sea.
15 Wherefore glorify ye the LORD in the east, even the name
of the LORD, the God of Israel, in the isles of the sea.
16   From the uttermost part of the earth have we heard
songs, glory to the righteous. But I said, I pine away, I
pine away, woe is me! the treacherous dealers have dealt

---

11. crying...wine: i.e. lamentation over the desolate vineyards.

13. The description of the premonitory signs of the coming
judgment (*vv.* 1-12) is followed by a prediction of the almost
total extermination of the human race. For the imagery see on
xvii. 6, of which this verse is an imitation.

14-16. This writer's gloomy views of the present and immediate
future were not shared by all his compatriots. From distant
lands came songs of triumph and exhortations to joy and
gratitude. What event, or series of events, gave rise to these
expressions of hope and gladness is not stated, and cannot be
conjectured. The suggestion that it may have been the vic-
torious march of Alexander is attractive, though without sub-
stantial foundation.

14. These: the Jews of the Diaspora in emphatic contrast to
' I,' *v.* 16*b*.

shall lift...shall shout: the tenses should be present.

15. in the east. The meaning is doubtful (cf. marg.), but the
rendering 'in the regions of light' (=the east or north-east) is
preferable to any of the suggested emendations.

isles: marg. ' coastlands.'

16. righteous: i.e. the righteous people, Israel; cf. xxvi. 2.

But...treacherously. The prophet can take no comfort from
any ordinary event, however apparently propitious. He faints
at the thought of the cruelty and oppression that will yet afflict

treacherously; yea, the treacherous dealers have dealt very treacherously.

17-20. *Catastrophic accompaniments of the judgment—*
deluge and earthquake.

Fear, and the pit, and the snare, are upon thee, O 17 inhabitant of the earth. And it shall come to pass, 18 that he who fleeth from the noise of the fear shall fall into the pit; and he that cometh up out of the midst of the pit shall be taken in the snare: for the windows on high are opened, and the foundations of the earth do shake. The earth is utterly broken, the earth is clean dissolved, 19 the earth is moved exceedingly. The earth shall stagger 20 like a drunken man, and shall be moved to and fro like a hut; and the transgression thereof shall be heavy upon it, and it shall fall, and not rise again.

21-23. *Judgment on the exalted powers of evil, and*
the enthronement of Yahwe in glory on Zion.

And it shall come to pass in that day, that the LORD 21 shall punish the host of the high ones on high, and the

---

the people before the decisive interposition of Yahwe delivers them.

17-20. The delineation of the judgment is resumed from *v.* 13. *Vv.* 17, 18*a* are repeated almost verbatim, but with special reference to Moab, in Jer. xlviii. 43.

18. windows...opened: cf. Gen. vii. 11.

19. the earth is clean...exceedingly: render 'the earth is shivered in pieces; the earth staggers and sways.'

20. hut: a light shelter, easily swayed by the wind. See i. 8 (lodge).

21-23. The judgment has two acts, (1) the defeat and imprisonment of the mundane and supramundane powers of evil; (2) their final punishment. The conception is similar to that in the book of Enoch and later apocalypses.

21. host...high: lit. 'the host of the height in the height' ='the host of heaven,' Jer. xxxiii. 22; Neh. ix. 6 (the stars); 1 Kings xxii. 19 (angels). Here possibly both stars, as objects of idolatrous worship, and angels, as patrons of earthly powers (cf. Dan. x. 13, 20 f.), are meant. The book of Enoch speaks of the imprisonment of the 'stars of heaven and the host of heaven.' Cf. also Eph. ii. 2, iii. 10; Col. i. 16.

22 kings of the earth upon the earth. And they shall be
gathered together, as prisoners are gathered in the pit,
and shall be shut up in the prison, and after many days
23 shall they be visited. Then the moon shall be confounded,
and the sun ashamed; for the LORD of hosts shall reign
in mount Zion, and in Jerusalem, and before his ancients
gloriously.

xxv. 1-5. *A song of praise.*

25   O LORD, thou art my God; I will exalt thee, I will
praise thy name; for thou hast done wonderful things,
2 *even* counsels of old, in faithfulness *and* truth. For thou
hast made of a city an heap; of a defenced city a ruin: a
palace of strangers to be no city; it shall never be built.
3 Therefore shall the strong people glorify thee, the city of
4 the terrible nations shall fear thee. For thou hast been a

---

22. shut up...visited: the hostile powers are imprisoned
beneath the earth to await their final judgment and punishment.
Cf. 2 Pet. ii. 4; Jude 6. A modification of the same conception
appears in Rev. xx.

23. Then...ashamed: the light of the sun and moon pales
and disappears before that of the Divine glory. (Cf. lx. 19 f.;
Rev. xxi. 23.)

before...gloriously: marg. 'before his elders (the heads of
the post-exilic community) shall be glory.'

Ch. xxv.

1-5. The psalmist gives expression to the gratitude of Yahwe's
people for their deliverance from peril, and for a signal defeat
inflicted on their enemies. None of the various conjectures
which have been made as to the identity of the city in *v.* 2,
or the events which suggested the psalm, is really plausible.

1. for thou...truth: 'for thou hast executed wonder-
counsels (cf. 'wonder-counsellor,' ix. 6), which from afar (i.e.
from the far-off days when the Divine purposes were formed,
or proclaimed through the prophets) were truth in faithfulness.'
The psalmist has witnessed the fulfilment of ancient prophecy.

2. palace of strangers: better 'fortress of the impious'
(LXX).

3. strong people...city: the expressions are probably col-
lective: 'many a strong people...many a city.'

strong hold to the poor, a strong hold to the needy in his
distress, a refuge from the storm, a shadow from the heat,
when the blast of the terrible ones is as a storm against
the wall. As the heat in a dry place shalt thou bring down 5
the noise of strangers ; as the heat by the shadow of a
cloud, the song of the terrible ones shall be brought low.

6–8. No sorrow mars the perfect bliss of Yahwe's reign.

And in this mountain shall the LORD of hosts make unto 6
all peoples a feast of fat things, a feast of wines on the
lees, of fat things full of marrow, of wines on the lees well
refined. And he will destroy in this mountain the face of 7
the covering that is cast over all peoples, and the veil
that is spread over all nations. He hath swallowed up 8
death for ever ; and the Lord GOD will wipe away tears

---

4. when...wall: read 'for the blast of the tyrants is as a
rain-storm in winter.' The clause is probably a gloss in explanation of the metaphor 'a refuge from the storm.'

5. The meaning is that Yahwe has protected His people
from the triumphant might of their enemies as an intervening
cloud protects the earth from the fierce heat of the sun. The
verse is intended to amplify and explain the metaphor 'a
shadow from the heat' (*v.* 4).

6–8. The continuation of xxiv. 23. Yahwe, enthroned in
glory on Zion, prepares a feast for all the peoples of the earth.
He admits them to His fellowship, removes every trace of
sorrow, and abolishes death itself. The writer's deep and
universal sympathy with suffering humanity makes the passage
one of the most beautiful and touching in the Bible.

6. feast of fat things...marrow. The royal banquet, at which
the choicest and richest portions (usually reserved at sacrificial
feasts for the Deity) are set before the guests, typifies the enjoy-
ment of the highest spiritual blessings.

wines...refined: strong pure wine which had been left on the
sediment for further fermentation and then strained.

7. covering...veil: the symbols of grief.

8. He hath...ever. In the perfectly blessed Messianic kingdom
there will be no death, and therefore no grief. This conception
finds its clearest expression in O.T. in this passage. The hope
of a resurrection of those already dead is a further development
of it (see on xxvi. 19). This abolition of death in the divine
kingdom must be distinguished from the Christian idea of the

from off all faces ; and the reproach of his people shall
he take away from off all the earth : for the LORD hath
spoken it.

9-12. *Israel's triumph over Moab.*

9   And it shall be said in that day, Lo, this is our God ;
we have waited for him, and he will save us : this is the
LORD ; we have waited for him, we will be glad and
10 rejoice in his salvation.   For in this mountain shall the
hand of the LORD rest, and Moab shall be trodden down
in his place, even as straw is trodden down in the water of
11 the dunghill.   And he shall spread forth his hands in the
midst thereof, as he that swimmeth spreadeth forth *his
hands* to swim : and he shall lay low his pride together
12 with the craft of his hands.   And the fortress of the high
fort of thy walls hath he brought down, laid low, and
brought to the ground, even to the dust.

xxvi. 1-19. *A psalm of praise and aspiration.*

26   In that day shall this song be sung in the land of Judah :

---

immortal spirit surviving the death of the body.   The quotation
in 1 Cor. xv. 54 gives the word for 'for ever' its Aramaic
sense of 'victory.'

the reproach of his people.   The Jews of the Dispersion
suffered already from the dislike of their Gentile neighbours,
while the contrast between their national aspirations and their
actual position was itself a reproach, which would be triumphantly
removed by the establishment of the divine kingdom.

9-12.   The song gives thanks for Yahwe's aid already given
(*v.* 9), and anticipates a crushing defeat of Moab.   The historical
occasion is unknown.

11.   pride : cf. xvi. 6; Zeph. ii. 8, 10.

together...hands.   The meaning of the word translated 'craft'
is quite uncertain.   The general sense is that in spite of all his
efforts Moab will be forced down into the dung-pit.

12.   This verse seems to belong rather to the context
xxvi. 5, 6, and may have been misplaced.

Ch. xxvi. 1-19.

The opening formula (*v.* 1a) implies that this psalm is
prophetic, that it is intended to voice the gratitude of the

We have a strong city ; salvation will he appoint for walls
and bulwarks. Open ye the gates, that the righteous 2
nation which keepeth truth may enter in. Thou wilt keep 3
him in perfect peace, *whose* mind *is* stayed *on thee*:
because he trusteth in thee. Trust ye in the LORD for 4
ever : for in the LORD JEHOVAH is an everlasting rock.
For he hath brought down them that dwell on high, the 5
lofty city : he layeth it low, he layeth it low even to the
ground ; he bringeth it even to the dust. The foot shall 6
tread it down ; even the feet of the poor, and the steps
of the needy. The way of the just is uprightness : 7
thou that art upright dost direct the path of the just.
Yea, in the way of thy judgements, O LORD, have 8
we waited for thee ; to thy name and to thy memorial is

---

redeemed community after the establishment of the divine
kingdom. This standpoint, however, is not maintained throughout the psalm. The writer's mood is one of mingled gratitude
and aspiration. Much has been won, but salvation is not yet
complete. The circumstances of the time are doubtless reflected
in the poem, which passes without clearly marked divisions
from praise for present deliverance to prayers for further
blessing, mingled with subdued retrospect of past sufferings,
closing on a note of confident and glorious hope. The introduction (*v.* 1 *a*) should therefore be regarded as editorial. There
are no explicit indications of date.

1. salvation...bulwarks : render 'for protection He (Yahwe)
sets walls and bulwarks,' the bulwark being a smaller
rampart in front of the main wall. The opening verses may
suggest that some restoration of the fortifications of Jerusalem
was the immediate occasion of the poem.

2. truth : fidelity to Yahwe.

3. Marg. 'a steadfast mind Thou keepest in perfect peace,
because it trusts in Thee.' 'Mind' (elsewhere, as Gen. vi. 5,
Deut. xxxi. 21, rendered 'imagination') means here disposition
or character.

4. for...rock : read 'for Yahwe (om. 'in the Lord') is an
everlasting rock.'

5. city : presumably the same as in xxv. 2. See on xxv. 1–5.

6. poor...needy : i.e. the Jews, as in xxv. 4. Cf. xiv. 30, 32.

7. uprightness : lit. 'straightness,' a smooth and easy road.
thou...just : read 'thou makest level the path of the just.'

8. memorial : synonymous with 'name,' as in Ex. iii. 15 ;

9 the desire of our soul.   With my soul have I desired thee
in the night ; yea, with my spirit within me will I seek
thee early : for when thy judgements are in the earth, the
10 inhabitants of the world learn righteousness.   Let favour
be shewed to the wicked, yet will he not learn righteousness ; in the land of uprightness will he deal wrongfully,
and will not behold the majesty of the LORD.

11   LORD, thy hand is lifted up, yet they see not : but they
shall see *thy* zeal for the people, and be ashamed ; yea,
12 fire shall devour thine adversaries.   LORD, thou wilt
ordain peace for us : for thou hast also wrought all our
13 works for us.   O LORD our God, other lords beside thee
have had dominion over us ; but by thee only will we make
14 mention of thy name.   *They are* dead, they shall not live ;

Ps. cxxxv. 13. That the name by which Yahwe had caused
Himself to be known and remembered should be held in
universal honour was the heartfelt desire of the faithful community.

9. early : marg. ‘ diligently.’

10. A prayer for further judgment on the heathen oppressors
(**the wicked**), who are not amenable to the Divine grace, and,
if still spared (‘ let favour...’=‘ if favour...’), will continue to
act impiously in the **land of uprightness,** i.e. the land of
Yahwe’s faithful people.

11. Yahwe’s hand has already been lifted up in judgment,
but the ‘ wicked ’ have not recognized it.

but...adversaries : read ‘ but they shall see (i.e. they shall be
compelled to recognize Yahwe’s hand), and be ashamed ; zeal
for Thy people (Yahwe’s zeal) and the fire of (i.e. directed
against) Thine adversaries shall consume them.’

12. thou hast...us : each deliverance has been wrought, and
every victory won, for us by Thee, and not by our own might.

13. other lords : i.e. the heathen empires, the domination of
which over Yahwe’s people was a limitation of His sovereignty.

but...name. The rendering ‘ by Thee...’ (=‘ by Thy help...’)
is forced, and the sense is unsatisfactory. The line is probably
defective. The idea is ‘ but now that Thou hast delivered us we
shall serve Thee only.’

14. They are dead...rise : marg. ‘ the dead live not, the
shades (see xiv. 9) rise not.’ The heathen lords have passed
away into the underworld, and can never return. The contrast
with *v.* 19 is striking. Both verses bring consolation, the one

they are deceased, they shall not rise : therefore hast thou
visited and destroyed them, and made all their memory to
perish.   Thou hast increased the nation, O LORD, thou 15
hast increased the nation ; thou art glorified : thou hast
enlarged all the borders of the land.

LORD, in trouble have they visited thee, they poured 16
out a prayer *when* thy chastening was upon them.   Like 17
as a woman with child, that draweth near the time of her
delivery, is in pain and crieth out in her pangs ; so have
we been before thee, O LORD.   We have been with child, 18
we have been in pain, we have as it were brought forth
wind ; we have not wrought any deliverance in the earth ;
neither have the inhabitants of the world fallen.   Thy 19

---

with the thought that the foreign despots share the universal
human fate of irrevocable death, the other with the assurance of a
great exception to the common lot in favour of the faithful Jews.

15.   The verse is neither a prophecy nor a prayer, but refers
to actual circumstances.   The deliverances from foreign domination which Yahwe has wrought for His people have extended
their territory.

thou art glorified : rather 'Thou hast glorified Thyself,'
every success of Israel bringing honour to Yahwe.

16-18.   After all, in spite of what has been accomplished,
achievement has been but slight, and the population of the land
is deplorably scanty.

16.   visited thee : rather ' sought Thee.'

they poured...them : a difficult clause as regards both vocabulary and grammar.   ' Prayer' should be ' enchantment'
(lit. ' whispering '), and ' they poured out' is hardly possible.
The rendering ' Thy chastisement was the constraint of enchantment to them,' i.e. ' compelled them as by a magic spell to turn
to Thee,' is both forced and doubtful.   The emendation ' they
cried out, when Thy chastisement oppressed them ' is preferable.

17.   The tribulation of the crisis through which deliverance
was wrought was like the agony of child-birth. (Cf. Hos. xiii. 13.)

18.   The metaphor of *v.* 17 suggests the almost despairing cry
that the agony has been vain—only wind (cf. Hos. xii. 1 ;
Eccles. i. 14 marg.) has been brought forth.

we have not...earth : we have not yet established peace and
prosperity in the land.

neither...fallen : marg. ' neither have inhabitants of the world
been born,' an unusual meaning of the word 'fall,' justified by

dead shall live ; my dead bodies shall arise. Awake and
sing, ye that dwell in the dust : for thy dew is *as* the dew
of herbs, and the earth shall cast forth the dead.

xxvi. 20–xxvii. 1.   *The seclusion of Israel during the execution
of the judgment.*

20   Come, my people, enter thou into thy chambers, and
shut thy doors about thee : hide thyself for a little moment,
21   until the indignation be overpast. For, behold, the LORD
cometh forth out of his place to punish the inhabitants of
the earth for their iniquity : the earth also shall disclose
her blood, and shall no more cover her slain.

27   In that day the LORD with his sore and great and
strong sword shall punish leviathan the swift serpent, and
leviathan the crooked serpent ; and he shall slay the
dragon that is in the sea.

---

the analogy of other languages, and by the context (see end
of *v.* 19).

19. The distresses and disappointments of the crisis are
forgotten in the hope of a miraculous resurrection which will
re-people the land with those who have died in faith.

Thy...my. The faithful belong both to Yahwe and Israel.

for...herbs: read 'for dew of lights (dew from the realm of
divine light) is Thy dew.' This wonderful dew will revivify the
dead.

cast forth the dead: rather 'bring shades to birth,' lit.
'cause shades to fall,' in the same sense as 'have fallen'='have
been born,' *v.* 18.

Ch. xxvi. 20–xxvii. 1.

21. the earth also...slain. The blood which has sunk into
the earth and been lost to sight will appear once more upon the
surface, and thus cry for vengeance (cf. Ezek. xxiv. 7 f.), and
buried bodies will be exposed to witness against the murderers.

xxvii. 1. Yahwe executes judgment on three heathen em-
pires, the identity of which is veiled in apocalyptic imagery.
The 'dragon that is in the sea' typifies Egypt (cf. Ezek. xxix. 3,
xxxii. 2). The leviathan (Job iii. 8), a creation probably of
Babylonian mythology, has here two forms, the 'fleeing serpent'
(Job xxvi. 13), and the 'coiled serpent.' The identification of the
two powers thus symbolized depends on the date of the passage.
They may have been e.g. the Persian and Greek Empires.

2-6. *A song of Yahwe's vineyard.*

In that day : A vineyard of wine, sing ye unto it.   I the ²⁄₃
LORD do keep it ; I will water it every moment ; lest any
hurt it, I will keep it night and day.   Fury is not in me : 4
would that the briers and thorns were against me in battle !
I would march upon them, I would burn them together.
Or else let him take hold of my strength, that he may 5
make peace with me ; *yea*, let him make peace with me.
In days to come shall Jacob take root ; Israel shall blossom 6
and bud : and they shall fill the face of the world with
fruit.

7-11. *An obscure fragment.*

Hath he smitten him as he smote those that smote him? 7
or is he slain according to the slaughter of them that were

Ch. xxvii. 2-6.

The song (*vv.* 2-5), which is without relation to its context,
expresses, in sharp contrast to the song of the vineyard in
v. 1-7, Yahwe's satisfaction with His vineyard, and His intention to protect it.   *V.* 6 is a prose addendum.

2.   Read 'in that day (it shall be said) "vineyard of delight
(see marg.)—sing ye of it."'   The introductory formula is
incomplete (see xxv. 9).

4. Fury...me: 'wrath I have not': i.e. Yahwe is no longer, as
in v. 5 ff., displeased with His vineyard.

would that...together.   The syntax is obscure, and the text
somewhat uncertain.   The meaning is 'should there be briers
and thorns in my vineyard I would march to battle against them
(an awkward mingling of metaphor and interpretation), and burn
them.'   The briers and thorns of v. 6 are here employed metaphorically of heathen oppressors intruding upon Yahwe's land.

5.   In obscure language the thought is expressed that the
heathen may escape destruction by submission to Yahwe.

6.   A prose appendix promising Israel a prosperous future.

7-11.   A very obscure passage of uncertain date.   It is a
fragment without apparent connection with any part of its
context.   (See introductory note to ch. xxiv.–xxvii.)

7. that were slain by him: read 'that slew him.'   The
rhetorical question is asked whether Yahwe's chastisement of
Israel was as severe as that inflicted on Israel's enemies, the
expected answer being 'no.'

8 slain by him? In measure, when thou sendest her away,
thou dost contend with her; he hath removed *her* with
9 his rough blast in the day of the east wind. Therefore by
this shall the iniquity of Jacob be purged, and this is all
the fruit of taking away his sin; when he maketh all the
stones of the altar as chalkstones that are beaten in sunder,
so that the Asherim and the sun-images shall rise no more.
10 For the defenced city is solitary, an habitation deserted
and forsaken, like the wilderness: there shall the calf feed,
and there shall he lie down, and consume the branches
11 thereof. When the boughs thereof are withered, they shall
be broken off; the women shall come, and set them on
fire: for it is a people of no understanding; therefore he
that made them will not have compassion upon them, and
he that formed them will shew them no favour.

---

8. The feminine pronouns indicate that a city is spoken of,
as in *v.* 10, to which this verse may be a gloss. **In measure**
means that the punishment was inflicted in carefully measured
quantities, but the rendering is extremely doubtful, and the
clause is altogether obscure. Read, possibly, 'by driving her
forth (as an animal is driven), by casting her out, Thou con-
tendedst with her.' The allusion is apparently to the exile, the
east wind in the second clause probably referring to the
Babylonians.

9. The condition of final forgiveness, and the result or aim
(**fruit**) of Yahwe's gracious dealing, is that the land should be
altogether purified from illegitimate worship.

  purged: marg. 'expiated.'

  when…altar: rather 'that he should make all altar-stones.'

  Asherim and the sun-images: see on xvii. 8.

10, 11. If the deserted city be the same as in xxv. 2, xxvi. 5,
these verses must be connected immediately with *v.* 7, and
emphasize the magnitude of the chastisement inflicted upon
Israel's enemies. But the context, and especially the language
of *v.* 11, 'a people of no understanding,' and 'he that formed
them,' indicate that Jerusalem is meant. The sin of the people
is not yet expiated, and until they show spiritual discernment
('understanding'), and truly turn to God, forsaking all false
worship (*v.* 9), He cannot fully deliver them. The tenses
should be present throughout.

12, 13. The great ingathering.

And it shall come to pass in that day, that the LORD 12
shall beat off *his fruit*, from the flood of the River unto
the brook of Egypt, and ye shall be gathered one by one,
O ye children of Israel.

And it shall come to pass in that day, that a great 13
trumpet shall be blown ; and they shall come which were
ready to perish in the land of Assyria, and they that were
outcasts in the land of Egypt ; and they shall worship the
LORD in the holy mountain at Jerusalem.

*xxviii. 1–22. A denunciation of the dissolute and ribald
priests and nobles of Jerusalem.*

1–6. The doom of Samaria.

Woe to the crown of pride of the drunkards of Ephraim, **28**
and to the fading flower of his glorious beauty, which is on

12, 13. These verses (with which cf. xi. 11, 12) are the natural
continuation of *v.* 1.   The ingathering of Israel follows the final
judgment on the heathen empires.
12. the Lord…Egypt: render ' Yahwe shall thresh out from
the corn-ears of the River (Euphrates) to the brook of Egypt '
(the Wady el-Arish).   Within these ideal limits of the territory
of Israel (Gen. xv. 18) Yahwe will beat out the grain (Jud. vi. 11),
and separate the corn (Israel) from the straw and chaff (the
heathen), taking care that no single grain is lost **(one by one)**.
13.   The faithful who are outside Yahwe's territory will be
brought into it.
trumpet.   The blowing of the trumpet became a constant
feature of eschatological pictures; cf. Matt. xxiv. 31; 1 Cor. xv.
52; 1 Thess. iv. 16.
they…which…perish: marg. 'the lost.'

Ch. xxviii.–xxxv. PROPHECIES RELATING CHIEFLY (xxviii.–
xxxi.) TO THE POLITICS OF JUDAH IN THE CRITICAL
YEARS IMMEDIATELY PRECEDING SENNACHERIB'S IN-
VASION (701 B.C.), AND MORE PARTICULARLY TO HEZE-
KIAH'S ALLIANCE WITH EGYPT.

The abrupt transitions in this group of oracles from threats of
judgment to promises of deliverance are somewhat puzzling, and
it is not surprising that they have given rise to suspicions of

the head of the fat valley of them that are overcome with
2 wine ! Behold, the Lord hath a mighty and strong one ;

extensive interpolation. The apparent inconsistency, however,
is characteristic of Isaiah's preaching throughout the book,
appearing in the contrast between such predictions of deliverance as x. 5-34, xvii. 12-14 and the constant and strongly
expressed warnings of approaching doom. It was observed and
criticized by Isaiah's opponents, as may be gathered from his
defence in the parable in xxviii. 23-29. Regarding the abruptness
of the transitions note (1) that oracles delivered at different
times may have been combined for literary purposes, e.g. perhaps
in the difficult cases xxix. 1-8, xxxi.: (2) that conditions change
rapidly in times of sharp crisis, and therefore, although the
oracles belong approximately to the same period, there was
probably considerable variety in the precise circumstances in
which each was delivered ; sometimes the emphasis lies on
the completeness of the approaching disaster, sometimes the
prophet's gaze is fixed on the deliverance that will succeed the
desolation : (3) that Isaiah's theory was that Yahwe would
utterly destroy the existing regime, and with it the bulk of the
people, using the Assyrians as His instruments for that purpose,
and would then Himself repel Assyria and rescue Jerusalem.
He fights, therefore, with the Assyrians against Judah, and then
against Assyria on behalf of His own ideal city and kingdom.
See on ch. xxxi.

The crucial feature of the crisis was the project of a revolt
against the Assyrian suzerainty, in reliance on the assistance of
Egypt. This scheme of the dominant party was denounced by
Isaiah as an act of political folly, amounting to suicide, and as a
renunciation of the one hope of safety—quiet confidence in
Yahwe, and obedience to His declared will.

The group of oracles xxviii.–xxxiii. in its present arrangement
is somewhat artificially divided into six passages each introduced
by the interjection 'Woe' or 'Ah' (xxviii. 1, xxix. 1, 15, xxx. 1,
xxxi. 1, xxxiii. 1).

I. Ch. xxviii. 1-22.

1-4. It is obvious that these verses were written before the fall
of Samaria (722 B.C.). They were incorporated with this context,
probably by Isaiah himself, as an introduction to the denunciation of similar vices in Judah (*vv.* 7-22).

1. Samaria, beautifully situated on a hill overlooking a
fertile valley, is likened to a chaplet of flowers on the head of
a reveller. But the wearer is a drunkard, and the flowers are
fading.

2. mighty...one: the Assyrian (cf. v. 26-29).

as a tempest of hail, a destroying storm, as a tempest of
mighty waters overflowing, shall he cast down to the earth
with the hand. The crown of pride of the drunkards of 3
Ephraim shall be trodden under foot : and the fading 4
flower of his glorious beauty, which is on the head of the
fat valley, shall be as the firstripe fig before the summer ;
which when he that looketh upon it seeth, while it is yet
in his hand he eateth it up. In that day shall the LORD 5
of hosts be for a crown of glory, and for a diadem of
beauty, unto the residue of his people : and for a spirit of 6
judgement to him that sitteth in judgement, and for
strength to them that turn back the battle at the gate.

7-13. *Isaiah's encounter with the drunken priests
and prophets.*

But these also have erred through wine, and through 7
strong drink are gone astray ; the priest and the prophet
have erred through strong drink, they are swallowed up
of wine, they are gone astray through strong drink ; they
err in vision, they stumble in judgement. For all tables 8

---

shall...hand : rather 'that hurls down to the earth with
violence' (lit. 'with the hand').

4. The early fig, ripening in June instead of in August, the
principal fig-season, was esteemed a choice delicacy (Mic. vii. 1 ;
Jer. xxiv. 2). As soon as such a fig was seen it was pounced
upon and eaten. Thus swiftly and greedily would the Assyrians
fall upon Samaria.

5, 6. A Messianic fragment, probably by a later hand. The
expressions in *vv.* 1, 3 are modified and applied to Yahwe
Himself, the glorious crown of His people in the Messianic
age (' in that day').

6. that...gate : that drive back the enemy already pouring
through the gate of the almost captured city.

7, 8. The connecting link between *vv.* 1-4 and *vv.* 9-13.
The vices and follies which brought ruin on Samaria are now
characteristic of the ruling classes of Jerusalem (**these also**).

7. they err...judgement : the effects of intemperate self-
indulgence ; the prophets were unable to interpret their own
visions, and the priests, in the exercise of their judicial functions
(Deut. xix. 17 ; Ezek. xliv. 24), gave faulty decisions.

are full of vomit *and* filthiness, *so that there is* no place
9 *clean.*   Whom will he teach knowledge? and whom will
he make to understand the message? them that are
10 weaned from the milk, and drawn from the breasts?   For
it is precept upon precept, precept upon precept; line
11 upon line, line upon line; here a little, there a little.   Nay,
but by *men of* strange lips and with another tongue will
12 he speak to this people: to whom he said, This is the
rest, give ye rest to him that is weary; and this is the
13 refreshing: yet they would not hear.   Therefore shall the
word of the LORD be unto them precept upon precept,
precept upon precept; line upon line, line upon line; here
a little, there a little; that they may go, and fall backward, and be broken, and snared, and taken.

---

8.   A description, probably, of an actual banquet at which
priests, prophets, and nobles were carousing.   When the orgy
is at its height Isaiah enters and expresses his abhorrence of the
scene.

9.   The scornful retort of the revellers.   Does the man take
us for babes?   Will he instruct us—the priests—in the knowledge of the divine law? or us—the prophets—how to interpret
that which we hear from Yahwe (**the message**)?

10.   In a series of unintelligible monosyllables—apparently
abbreviations of longer words—each repeated twice, the revellers
caricature, with the indistinct utterance of intoxication, the
prophet's monotonous reiteration of elementary truths.

line (measuring-line): marg. 'rule.'

11.   Isaiah throws back the taunt: 'you stammer out strange
words; you will soon hear strange words indeed, that will sound
in your ears like unintelligible stammering,' i.e. the tongue of
the Assyrians, Yahwe's instruments.

12.   to whom he said: rather 'He who said to them.'

This is the rest…refreshing: possibly 'this (Jerusalem) is (or
ideally should be) the place of rest…and of refreshment'; but
more probably 'this (the quiet faith inculcated by the teaching
which you ridicule) is the true rest…and refreshment.'   Cf.
xxx. 15.

him…weary: the peasant who bore the brunt of the toil and
privation entailed by the foolish policy of revolt.

13.   The mocking caricature of the **word of Yahwe** through
the prophet (*v.* 10) will be a grim reality when Yahwe speaks
in a monotonous reiteration of punitive judgments.

14-22. A warning to the scoffing politicians.

Wherefore hear the word of the LORD, ye scornful men, 14
that rule this people which is in Jerusalem : Because ye 15
have said, We have made a covenant with death, and with
hell are we at agreement ; when the overflowing scourge
shall pass through, it shall not come unto us ; for we have
made lies our refuge, and under falsehood have we hid
ourselves : therefore thus saith the Lord GOD, Behold, I 16
lay in Zion for a foundation a stone, a tried stone, a
precious corner *stone* of sure foundation : he that believeth
shall not make haste. And I will make judgement the 17
line, and righteousness the plummet : and the hail shall
sweep away the refuge of lies, and the waters shall over-

14-22. This section is similar in substance to what precedes,
and is connected with it by the opening word. But it is probable
that the recriminations at the banquet close at *v.* 13, and that
vv. 14-22 give the substance of another address delivered about
the same time.

14. scornful men : 'scoffers' (*v.* 22, xxix. 20), the religious
and political leaders of the people, who received Yahwe's message
through His prophet with open ridicule and contempt.

15. That the words 'lies' and 'falsehood' are put into the
mouths of the 'scoffers' shows that Isaiah is reproducing their
reckless boast according to his own interpretation of its real
meaning.   How they themselves would have described the
'covenant with death' and the 'agreement with Sheol' (not
'hell') cannot be guessed. The allusion is doubtless to the
practice of necromancy (viii. 19).

overflowing scourge. The striking mixture of metaphor is
more than paralleled in *v.* 18.

16. I lay : rather 'I have laid.'

stone. The costly foundation stone laid by Yahwe is His own
relation to Israel and His Divine purpose and will as revealed
through the prophet. Discernment of the Divine will and
obedience to it, and not superstitious practices or political
alliances are the basis of real security.

make haste : read 'give way.' Faith (see on vii. 9) is the
supreme condition of salvation and security.

17. The building erected on the invisible but sure foundation
(*v.* 16), with justice and righteousness for measuring-line and
plummet, will stand when the storm sweeps away the flimsy
structure reared on lies. Cf. Matt. vii. 24-27.

18 flow the hiding place. And your covenant with death
   shall be disannulled, and your agreement with hell shall
   not stand ; when the overflowing scourge shall pass
19 through, then ye shall be trodden down by it. As often
   as it passeth through, it shall take you ; for morning by
   morning shall it pass through, by day and by night : and
   it shall be nought but terror to understand the message.
20 For the bed is shorter than that a man can stretch himself
   on it ; and the covering narrower than that he can wrap
21 himself in it. For the LORD shall rise up as in mount
   Perazim, he shall be wroth as in the valley of Gibeon ;
   that he may do his work, his strange work, and bring to
22 pass his act, his strange act. Now therefore be ye not
   scorners, lest your bands be made strong : for a consummation, and that determined, have I heard from the Lord,
   the LORD of hosts, upon the whole earth.

23-29.   *A parable from husbandry.*

23   Give ye ear, and hear my voice ; hearken, and hear my

---

18. disannulled: 'obliterated,' an unparalleled use of the
regular word for 'expiate.' Read, perhaps, 'broken.'
19. The blow will fall not once nor twice only. The Divine
warnings (**message** as in *v.* 9) will be so persistent and
unmistakable that even the drunken prophets (*vv.* 7-13) will
hear and understand with unrelieved horror.
20. The priests and politicians had made an uncomfortable
bed for themselves. Now they must lie on it.
21. mount Perazim : see 2 Sam. v. 20 (Baal-perazim).
Gibeon : see 2 Sam. v. 25 (Geba) = 1 Chron. xiv. 16 (Gibeon).
strange. The strangeness consisted in the fact that Yahwe
was now to fight against Israel. In the past His people had
gained great victories by His aid ; now His hand was against
them.
22. bands: the cords that bind you, and make escape from
the approaching doom impossible.
consummation : see x. 23.

II. Ch. xxviii. 23-29.

In this parable Isaiah defends Yahwe and himself against the
charge of inconsistency. Consider the variety of the farmer's

speech. Doth the plowman plow continually to sow? 24
doth he *continually* open and break the clods of his
ground? When he hath made plain the face thereof, doth 25
he not cast abroad the fitches, and scatter the cummin,
and put in the wheat in rows and the barley in the
appointed place and the spelt in the border thereof?
For his God doth instruct him aright, *and* doth teach him. 26
For the fitches are not threshed with a sharp *threshing* 27
instrument, neither is a cart wheel turned about upon the
cummin; but the fitches are beaten out with a staff, and
the cummin with a rod. Bread *corn* is ground; for he 28
will not ever be threshing it: and though the wheel of his
cart and his horses scatter it, he doth not grind it. This 29
also cometh forth from the LORD of hosts, which is
wonderful in counsel, and excellent in wisdom.

---

operations. (1) He does not spend all his time ploughing; in
due season and in the right manner he sows various kinds of
seed (24 f.). (2) When threshing he takes account of the
differences in strength and quality between the various kinds of
grain, and uses in each case a suitable implement (27 f.). The
mingling of threat and promise in Isaiah's preaching is no real
inconsistency. Judgment does not continue for ever; it is
followed by salvation and newness of life. In executing His
judgments God does not treat all nations and all individuals
alike—Samaria may fall, while Jerusalem is delivered, the
impenitent may perish, while the 'Remnant' is saved. This
is not due to partiality or inconsistency on God's part, but to
differences of character in the nations or individuals themselves.

24. to sow: i.e. the object of ploughing being to prepare for
sowing. Omit as an awkward gloss.

25. fitches: marg. 'black cummin.'

in rows...in the appointed place: two words of doubtful
meaning, wanting in LXX. Omit as textual errors.

27. The threshing-sledge (**sharp instrument**) or the waggon
with sharp-edged wheels (**cart wheel**) would crush the cummin
altogether. It is therefore threshed with a flail.

28. Heavier implements are used for the coarser grain, but it
also is threshed, not crushed. Read 'Is bread-corn crushed?
Nay, he does not continually thresh it, but when he has driven
his cart-wheel over it, he scatters it (tosses it up that the wind
may carry away the chaff), without crushing it.'

29. The thought of *v.* 26 is repeated. The skill and know-

xxix. 1–8. *The sore distress and deliverance of Jerusalem.*

29   Ho Ariel, Ariel, the city where David encamped ! add
2 ye year to year ; let the feasts come round : then will I
distress Ariel, and there shall be mourning and lamen-
3 tation : and she shall be unto me as Ariel.   And I will
camp against thee round about, and will lay siege against
thee with a fort, and I will raise siege works against thee.
4 And thou shalt be brought down, and shalt speak out of
the ground, and thy speech shall be low out of the dust ;
and thy voice shall be as of one that hath a familiar spirit,
out of the ground, and thy speech shall whisper out of the
5 dust.   But the multitude of thy foes shall be like small

---

ledge of the husbandman come ultimately from God, who (this is
the implication) applies the same delicate variety of method to
the government of the world.

III. Ch. xxix. 1–8.

A threat of drastic judgment (*vv.* 1–4), and a promise of
sudden and complete deliverance (*vv.* 5–8).   The transition is
unexpected and abrupt, but not inexplicable in view of Isaiah's
general attitude at this crisis.   See introductory note to xxviii.–
xxxv.

1.   Ariel : i.e. 'altar-hearth,' as in Ezek. xliii. 15 (marg.).
The word is found in this sense also on the Moabite Stone.
The *prima facie* more natural explanation 'lion of God' is
unsuitable in this context (see *v.* 2).

add...round.   The occasion of the discourse was probably the
Feast of Tabernacles, the last of the annual series of festivals
(Ex. xxxiv. 22).   For a few years more the cycle of feasts and
fasts would be observed, and then the blow would fall.

2.   she...Ariel.   In the day of her distress Jerusalem will be
like an altar-hearth, reeking with the blood of her slain defenders.
The blood of the sacrificial victims on the altar doubtless suggested
the name Ariel, ominous of the bloody sacrifices of war and
siege.

4.   Jerusalem will be humbled to the dust, and her voice, no
longer loud in joyous celebration of the recurring festivals, will
be like that of a ghost, which, under the spell of the necro-
mancer, mutters from the ground.   See viii. 19.

5.   When the utter futility of political scheming and armed

dust, and the multitude of the terrible ones as chaff that passeth away : yea, it shall be at an instant suddenly. She shall be visited of the LORD of hosts with thunder, 6 and with earthquake, and great noise, with whirlwind and tempest, and the flame of a devouring fire. And the 7 multitude of all the nations that fight against Ariel, even all that fight against her and her strong hold, and that distress her, shall be as a dream, a vision of the night. And it shall be as when an hungry man dreameth, and, 8 behold, he eateth ; but he awaketh, and his soul is empty : or as when a thirsty man dreameth, and, behold, he drinketh ; but he awaketh, and, behold, he is faint, and his soul hath appetite : so shall the multitude of all the nations be, that fight against mount Zion.

9-12. Blind unintelligence the consequence of unbelief.

Tarry ye and wonder; take your pleasure and be 9 blind : they are drunken, but not with wine ; they

---

resistance has become evident Yahwe Himself, who till then has fought against Jerusalem (*v.* 3), intervenes to deliver.

terrible ones : 'tyrants.'

5*b***, 6. yea...visited :** read 'yea, of a sudden, suddenly, she shall be visited '—in mercy and not in judgment, as the immediate context shows.

thunder...fire : cf. xxx. 27 f., 30.

8. A modification of the metaphor of the evanescent dream (*v.* 7). The Assyrians are now themselves the dreamers; having dreamed that success was in their grasp they awake to disillusionment and despair.

IV. Ch. xxix. 9-14.

Two short passages, without special connection with what precedes, describing the spiritual torpor and insincerity which prevented the people from understanding and obeying the prophet's admonitions.

9. Tarry...blind : marg. 'be ye amazed, and wonder; blind yourselves and be blind.'

they are drunken...they stagger : LXX, better, 'be drunken...stagger.'

10 stagger, but not with strong drink.   For the LORD hath
poured out upon you the spirit of deep sleep, and hath
closed your eyes, the prophets ; and your heads, the seers,
11 hath he covered.   And all vision is become unto you as
the words of a book that is sealed, which men deliver to
one that is learned, saying, Read this, I pray thee : and
12 he saith, I cannot, for it is sealed : and the book is
delivered to him that is not learned, saying, Read this, I
pray thee : and he saith, I am not learned.

13, 14.   *The punishment of a merely formal worship.*

13   And the Lord said, Forasmuch as this people draw
nigh *unto me*, and with their mouth and with their lips do
honour me, but have removed their heart far from me,
and their fear of me is a commandment of men which
14 hath been taught *them* : therefore, behold, I will proceed
to do a marvellous work among this people, even a

----

10.   The lack of understanding which is the result of self-
willed indifference to the Divine revelation is ascribed to the
action of Yahwe Himself; He has ordained the spiritual law
of which this is an example.   See on vi. 9, 10.

prophets...seers: two misleading glosses.   Yahwe has closed
the people's eyes, and covered their heads, so that they cannot
see or understand.

11, 12.   A revelation of all that is to befall them (R.V.,
wrongly, 'all vision') has been granted to the people through
Isaiah, but owing to the deep spiritual sleep which has overcome them they cannot understand it.   His message is like a
sealed book which the unlearned masses cannot read, while
their natural leaders and teachers, who could read if they would,
refuse to break the seal.

13.   **draw...mouth**: read 'draw nigh (unto Me) with their
mouth.'

mouth...lips...heart.   The liturgical formulae were correctly
recited, but the heart, the seat of genuine religious feeling, was
cold and unmoved.

and their fear...taught them.   Their religion was a matter of
custom and tradition, of observances prescribed by men.   They
had not entered with the heart into the Divine fellowship, and
learnt from God Himself.

marvellous work and a wonder: and the wisdom of their
wise men shall perish, and the understanding of their
prudent men shall be hid.

xxix. 15–xxxi.   *The league with Egypt.*

15–24.   *The politicians versus Yahwe.*

Woe unto them that seek deep to hide their counsel 15
from the LORD, and their works are in the dark, and they
say, Who seeth us? and who knoweth us? Ye turn 16
things upside down! Shall the potter be counted as
clay; that the thing made should say of him that made
it, He made me not; or the thing framed say of him
that framed it, He hath no understanding? Is it not 17
yet a very little while, and Lebanon shall be turned into

---

14. marvellous...wonder: cf. xxviii. 21. The deluded com-
placency of formal worship will be rudely shattered when Yahwe
reveals Himself in a manner not to be mistaken.
be hid: rather 'hide itself' in shame.

V. Ch. xxix. 15–xxxi.

xxix. 15–24. The passage opens with a reference to the
projected alliance with Egypt, at this stage still a secret intrigue,
and proceeds to contrast with this feeble scheme the great purpose
of Yahwe to establish in His own way His kingdom of peace and
blessedness. In tone and vocabulary *vv.* 17–24 resemble post-
exilic writings, and it is probable that the oracle was remodelled
by a later hand.
15. that...Lord: 'that hide a plan deep from Yahwe.' The
promoters of the Egyptian alliance had taken pains to conceal
the design from Isaiah, and had endeavoured to ignore his
revelation of the Divine will.
16. Ye...down: marg. 'O your perversity!'
Shall...understanding. For the figure of the potter and the
clay cf. xlv. 9, lxiv. 8; and also x. 15 for a similar thought
under another image.
17. See xxxii. 15. **Lebanon** was the typical forest, so that
we have here a simple interchange of forest and fruitful field,

a fruitful field, and the fruitful field shall be counted for a
18 forest? And in that day shall the deaf hear the words of
the book, and the eyes of the blind shall see out of
19 obscurity and out of darkness. The meek also shall
increase their joy in the LORD, and the poor among men
20 shall rejoice in the Holy One of Israel. For the terrible
one is brought to nought, and the scorner ceaseth, and all
21 they that watch for iniquity are cut off: that make a man
an offender in a cause, and lay a snare for him that
reproveth in the gate, and turn aside the just with a thing
22 of nought. Therefore thus saith the LORD, who redeemed
Abraham, concerning the house of Jacob: Jacob shall
not now be ashamed, neither shall his face now wax pale.
23 But when he seeth his children, the work of mine hands,
in the midst of him, they shall sanctify my name ; yea,
they shall sanctify the Holy One of Jacob, and shall
24 stand in awe of the God of Israel. They also that err in
spirit shall come to understanding, and they that murmur
shall learn doctrine.

---

whereas in xxxii. 15, probably the original form of the saying,
there is a gradation of luxuriance—wilderness, field, forest.

18. book: the revelation of God, with special reference to
the sealed book of *v.* 11. For spiritual deafness and blindness
cf. xlii. 18.

19. meek...poor: i.e. the humbly pious, as in many Psalms,
e.g. Ps. xiv. 6, xxxv. 10.

20. terrible one...scorner: the foreign tyrant and the Jewish
scoffer. See xxv. 4, xxviii. 14.

watch for iniquity: i.e. are on the look-out for an opportunity
to work mischief.

21. make...cause: secure the condemnation of the innocent.

22. who redeemed Abraham: an allusion to a late Jewish
story of the deliverance of Abraham from persecution in 'Ur of
the Chaldees.' A gloss, unless the whole verse be late.

23. when...hands: 'when he (i.e. Jacob=the people) sees
the work of my hands,' omitting 'his children' as a gloss.

xxx. 1–7.   *The futility of the alliance.*

Woe to the rebellious children, saith the LORD, that **30**
take counsel, but not of me; and that cover with a
covering, but not of my spirit, that they may add sin to
sin: that walk to go down into Egypt, and have not asked **2**
at my mouth; to strengthen themselves in the strength
of Pharaoh, and to trust in the shadow of Egypt! There- **3**
fore shall the strength of Pharaoh be your shame, and
the trust in the shadow of Egypt your confusion. For **4**
his princes are at Zoan, and his ambassadors are come to
Hanes. They shall all be ashamed of a people that **5**
cannot profit them, that are not an help nor profit, but a
shame, and also a reproach.

---

xxx. 1–7. Two short pieces, (*a*) *vv.* 1–5, (*β*) *vv.* 6, 7, having
the same theme, the second being parallel to the first, and not
its direct continuation. Ambassadors have started for Egypt,
now mentioned by name, to ask for Egyptian assistance in the
projected revolt against Assyria. Isaiah warns the people that
their hopes are illusory.

1. rebellious children: see i. 2.

that take counsel: rather 'that carry out a plan.'

and that...covering: probably 'that pour out a drink-
offering,' a ritual act accompanying the conclusion of a treaty.
But the meaning of the clause is doubtful (see marg.).

of my spirit: rather 'with my spirit,' according to my revealed
will.

2. to strengthen...Egypt: render 'to take refuge in the
refuge of Pharaoh, and to hide in the shadow of Egypt'; with
corresponding changes also in *v.* 3.

4, 5. Zoan (see xix. 11) and **Hanes** (identified with Heracle-
opolis magna, the modern Ahnas, somewhat south of Memphis)
are mentioned probably as well-known towns roughly marking
the limits of Pharaoh's territory in Lower Egypt. The sense
seems to be that Egypt, though perhaps imposing in size, is
utterly powerless to render effective assistance against Assyria.
Render 'for though his princes (perhaps 'vassals') are at Zoan,
and his messengers at Hanes (i.e. his authority is acknowledged
there), yet all (who trust him) are brought to shame through a
people....'

6   The burden of the beasts of the South.

Through the land of trouble and anguish, from whence
come the lioness and the lion, the viper and fiery flying
serpent, they carry their riches upon the shoulders of
young asses, and their treasures upon the bunches of
7 camels, to a people that shall not profit *them*.   For Egypt
helpeth in vain, and to no purpose: therefore have I
called her Rahab that sitteth still.

8-17.   *The consequences of unbelief and disobedience.*

8 Now go, write it before them on a tablet, and inscribe
it in a book, that it may be for the time to come for ever
9 and ever.   For it is a rebellious people, lying children,
10 children that will not hear the law of the LORD: which

---

6.   The burden...South: 'the oracle "beasts of the south,"'
an editorial title suggested, if the text be sound, by the mention
of so many animals in *v.* 6.

South: the Negeb, the desert south of ¡Judah, which the
ambassadors had to traverse on their way to Egypt.

fiery flying serpent : see vi. 2.

riches...treasures : gifts to the Pharaoh and his vassals.

7.   Rahab...still :   an utterly enigmatic expression, lit.
'Rahab they a sitting still.'   Rahab (from a root meaning
arrogance or violence), the name of a fabulous sea-monster
(Job xxvi. 12), became a symbolic designation of Egypt (cf.
li. 9; Ps. lxxxvii. 4, lxxxix. 10; and see on xxviii. 1).   The
phrase is doubtless contemptuous—perhaps 'Rahab Sit-still'—
'the blatant monster Do-nothing'—but the text is certainly
corrupt.

8.   write it.   What Isaiah was commanded to write is not
stated.   It may have been simply the enigmatic phrase in *v.* 7,
like Maher-shalal-hash-baz in viii. 1; but the mention of a
'book' suggests a longer document, and the circumstances recall
rather those of viii. 16.   Now, as then, Isaiah's words are unheeded by the people, and he is instructed to write down the
substance of his teaching—in this case his protests and warnings
regarding the Egyptian alliance.

for ever and ever: marg. 'for a witness for ever.'

9.   law : see on i. 10.

say to the seers, See not; and to the prophets, Prophesy
not unto us right things, speak unto us smooth things,
prophesy deceits: get you out of the way, turn aside out 11
of the path, cause the Holy One of Israel to cease from
before us.   Wherefore thus saith the Holy One of Israel, 12
Because ye despise this word, and trust in oppression and
perverseness, and stay thereon; therefore this iniquity 13
shall be to you as a breach ready to fall, swelling out in a
high wall, whose breaking cometh suddenly at an instant.
And he shall break it as a potter's vessel is broken, 14
breaking it in pieces without sparing; so that there shall
not be found among the pieces thereof a sherd to take
fire from the hearth, or to take water withal out of the
cistern.   For thus said the Lord GOD, the Holy One of 15
Israel, In returning and rest shall ye be saved; in
quietness and in confidence shall be your strength: and

---

10. which say...smooth things. It is a constant complaint of
the true prophets, who delivered their message faithfully and
fearlessly, that the people refused to listen to unpalatable truths,
and that there never lacked false prophets who pandered to their
taste for 'smooth things.' Cf. Amos ii. 12, vii. 12; Hos. ix. 7 f.;
Mic. ii. 6, 11, iii. 5; Jer. vi. 14, xiv. 13 f.

deceits. Isaiah makes the people express his own view of the
matter, as in xxviii. 15.

11. get...path: i.e. get out of your groove, drop your stern
and uncompromising tone.

cause...us: give us a rest from this everlasting talk about the
Holy One! The people were tired of Isaiah's constant insistence
on the ethical and spiritual character of Yahwe's relationship to
Israel.

12. this word: God's message through Isaiah.

oppression and perverseness: read 'obliquity and perversity,'
the crooked ways of political intrigue, and self-willed disobedience to God.

13, 14. The insidious process of moral declension, leading to
final ruin.   The cracked wall gradually bulges out until it falls
with a sudden crash (*v.* 13), which disintegrates it utterly and
irretrievably (*v.* 14).

15. In returning...strength: i.e. strength and safety lie in
the abandonment of your political and military schemes, in the

16 ye would not. But ye said, No, for we will flee upon
   horses; therefore shall ye flee: and, We will ride upon
   the swift; therefore shall they that pursue you be swift.
17 One thousand *shall flee* at the rebuke of one; at the
   rebuke of five shall ye flee: till ye be left as a beacon
   upon the top of a mountain, and as an ensign on an hill.

18–26. *Divine grace and guidance.*

18 And therefore will the LORD wait, that he may be
   gracious unto you, and therefore will he be exalted, that
   he may have mercy upon you: for the LORD is a God of
   judgement; blessed are all they that wait for him.
19   For the people shall dwell in Zion at Jerusalem: thou
   shalt weep no more; he will surely be gracious unto thee
   at the voice of thy cry; when he shall hear, he will
20 answer thee. And though the Lord give you the bread
   of adversity and the water of affliction, yet shall not thy
   teachers be hidden any more, but thine eyes shall see thy
21 teachers: and thine ears shall hear a word behind thee,
   saying, This is the way, walk ye in it; when ye turn to

---

avoidance of agitation and revolt, and in unperturbed reliance on
Yahwe.

16. flee: in the first clause transl. ' fly' (at the foe).

17.   The battle-cry of a handful of Assyrians will put the
boasters to ignominious flight.

beacon: rather 'flag-staff' (cf. marg.).

18–26. The style and spirit of this passage suggest that it,
like xxix. 17–24, is the product of a later age than Isaiah's.

18. And therefore...you: a promise of grace ('Yahwe is
eager to be gracious'), the beginning of an oracle of comfort and
promise, not, as in R.V., the concluding threat ('Yahwe will
delay being gracious') of the preceding denunciation.

19. For...Jerusalem: rather 'for, O people in Zion, that
dwellest in Jerusalem.'

20 f. Political and economic calamities may reduce the
faithful community to extreme distress, but it will not lose the
sense of the Divine presence and guidance.

20. yet...more: transl. (cf. marg.) ' yet thy Teacher (Yahwe)
shall no more hide Himself.'

21.   word: the voice of Yahwe directing His people's steps.

the right hand, and when ye turn to the left. And ye shall 22
defile the overlaying of thy graven images of silver, and
the plating of thy molten images of gold: thou shalt cast
them away as an unclean thing; thou shalt say unto it,
Get thee hence. And he shall give the rain of thy seed, 23
that thou shalt sow the ground withal; and bread of the
increase of the ground, and it shall be fat and plenteous:
in that day shall thy cattle feed in large pastures. The 24
oxen likewise and the young asses that till the ground
shall eat savoury provender, which hath been winnowed
with the shovel and with the fan. And there shall be 25
upon every lofty mountain, and upon every high hill,
rivers *and* streams of waters, in the day of the great
slaughter, when the towers fall. Moreover the light of 26
the moon shall be as the light of the sun, and the light of
the sun shall be sevenfold, as the light of seven days, in
the day that the LORD bindeth up the hurt of his people,
and healeth the stroke of their wound.

27-33. *The annihilation of the Assyrians by
Yahwe in person.*

Behold, the name of the LORD cometh from far, burning 27

---

22. The abandonment of idolatry (cf. xxvii. 9). The cover-
ings of precious metal with which images were overlaid would
be torn off, defiled (that they might lose all sacredness), and
scattered (marg.), thrown aside with disgust.

23-26. The enrichment of nature under the Divine blessing.

24. savoury provender: rather 'salted fodder,' esteemed a
delicacy for cattle.

25, 26. The language becomes eschatological. The 'day of
the great slaughter' is the great 'Day of Yahwe' (see ii. 12 ff.),
on which He comes forth to execute judgment on the world.
After that consummation there will be water-courses even on
dry heights, and sun and moon will shine with sevenfold
splendour.

26. as the light of seven days: omit, with LXX.

27. name of the Lord: the 'name of Yahwe' (= His glory,
Ps. cii. 15) means probably His personal manifestation of
Himself. In later times the mention of 'Yahwe' was avoided,
out of reverence, and 'the Name' was frequently substituted.

from far: perhaps from Seir or Sinai (Deut. xxxiii. 2;

with his anger, and in thick rising smoke: his lips are full
28 of indignation, and his tongue is as a devouring fire: and
his breath is as an overflowing stream, that reacheth even
unto the neck, to sift the nations with the sieve of vanity:
and a bridle that causeth to err *shall be* in the jaws of the
29 peoples.   Ye shall have a song as in the night when a
holy feast is kept; and gladness of heart, as when one
goeth with a pipe to come into the mountain of the LORD,
30 to the Rock of Israel.   And the LORD shall cause his
glorious voice to be heard, and shall shew the lighting
down of his arm, with the indignation of *his* anger, and
the flame of a devouring fire, with a blast, and tempest,
31 and hailstones.   For through the voice of the LORD shall
the Assyrian be broken in pieces, which smote with a rod.
32 And every stroke of the appointed staff, which the LORD
shall lay upon him, shall be with tabrets and harps: and

Jud. v. 4), but more probably the expression is intentionally
vague.   From its distant abode the transcendent glory suddenly
appears on the horizon.

28.   to sift...vanity: 'to swing the peoples in the sieve of
destruction.'

bridle...err.   Yahwe, in working out His purposes, turns the
Assyrians into what is for them the wrong path, that which leads
to their ruin.

29.   Ye...kept.   Songs of joy will be sung by the Israelites, as
on a festival evening (marg. 'when a feast is hallowed'), perhaps
the Passover evening, in which, in later times at least, singing
accompanied the feast (Matt. xxvi. 30).

as when...Israel: i.e. as on the occasion of a festal pro-
cession to the Temple.

30.   his glorious voice : i.e. His majestic thunder.

31.   which...rod: perhaps 'with a rod will he be smitten';
or the clause as it stands may be a gloss from x. 34.

32.   A difficult verse, the expressions 'appointed staff' and
'battles of shaking' (i.e. shaking of Yahwe's rod) being particularly
obscure.   Recent critics prefer to read 'and every stroke of
the staff shall be his (Assyria's) chastisement; to the sound of
tabrets and harps and with battles of wave-offering ('shaking,'
a technical term, as in Lev. vii. 30) will he fight with them,' the
idea being that Assyria is ritually devoted, like a sacrificial
victim, to destruction.

in battles of shaking will he fight with them. For a **33**
Topheth is prepared of old; yea, for the king it is made
ready; he hath made it deep and large: the pile thereof
is fire and much wood; the breath of the LORD, like a
stream of brimstone, doth kindle it.

xxxi. *The utter helplessness of Jerusalem, and its rescue by Yahwe.*

Woe to them that go down to Egypt for help, and stay **31**
on horses; and trust in chariots, because they are many,
and in horsemen, because they are very strong; but they
look not unto the Holy One of Israel, neither seek the
LORD! Yet he also is wise, and will bring evil, and will **2**
not call back his words: but will arise against the house of

---

33. The Assyrians will be slaughtered as human victims are
offered on an altar of fire to Moloch.

For...old: 'for a place of burning (Tophet) is already prepared.' Tophet, the spot in the valley of Hinnom where
human sacrifices were offered to Moloch, has here the generic
sense of burning-place.

yea...ready: the word for 'king' is the same as the name
Melek or Moloch, and it is not clear in this case whether it
means the king (of Assyria) or the god. Probably the latter is
meant, and the clause is a gloss suggested by the word Tophet.

xxxi. The allies, Judah and Egypt, are powerless to resist
Yahwe (*vv.* 1-4), who, however, will Himself defeat the
Assyrians and protect Jerusalem.

The guiding thought is that Yahwe is absolutely master of the
situation. Judah and Egypt on the one hand, and Assyria on
the other, are alike helpless before Him while He executes His
purpose of chastisement and deliverance.

1. The Jews were acutely conscious of their weakness
in the cavalry arm, and felt that if this were made good by the
help of Egypt they could defy Assyria. Isaiah's view was that
the one hope of safety lay in humble and obedient faith in
Yahwe. To him, therefore, reliance on cavalry meant, in
effect, disloyalty to Yahwe. Cf. ii. 7, xxx. 15, 16.

2. Yet...wise: ironical, 'you make clever plans; have you
not forgotten that God can also form and execute a purpose?'

and will bring...words: render 'and brings trouble (to those
who ignore Him), and has not recalled His words (the threats
communicated by the prophet).'

the evil-doers, and against the help of them that work
3 iniquity. Now the Egyptians are men, and not God; and
their horses flesh, and not spirit: and when the LORD
shall stretch out his hand, both he that helpeth shall
stumble, and he that is holpen shall fall, and they all shall
4 fail together. For thus saith the LORD unto me, Like as
when the lion growleth and the young lion over his prey,
if a multitude of shepherds be called forth against him, he
will not be dismayed at their voice, nor abase himself for
the noise of them: so shall the LORD of hosts come down
5 to fight upon mount Zion, and upon the hill thereof. As
birds flying, so will the LORD of hosts protect Jerusalem;
he will protect and deliver *it*, he will pass over and pre-
6 serve *it*. Turn ye unto him from whom ye have deeply
7 revolted, O children of Israel. For in that day they
shall cast away every man his idols of silver, and his idols
of gold, which your own hands have made unto you for

help: i.e. Egypt.

3. The spiritual transcends the material, and spiritual power
is concentrated in the one God. Those who range themselves
against Him perish inevitably.

he that helpeth...he that is holpen: Egypt and Judah.

4. The verse may possibly be interpreted to mean that
Yahwe will protect Jerusalem against the Assyrians as a lion
guards his booty from the shepherds. But assuming that the
simile is really forcible and pointed it must mean that Zion
is Yahwe's prey, which he seizes with violence from the shepherds
(its earthly rulers and their allies), undismayed by their noisy
boasts. That is, Yahwe, using the Assyrians as His instruments, will take Jerusalem out of the hands of its present
guardians. His purpose, however, is not to let it pass into
the possession of the Assyrians, but to keep it for Himself
(*v.* 5).

upon: marg. 'against.' The phrase is always used in a
hostile sense.

5. Yahwe protects Jerusalem as parent birds hover over
their nests.

6, 7. A summons to repentance in preparation for the day
when Yahwe will appear in judgment, and all idols will be cast
aside as useless (cf. ii. 20). The verses interrupt the context,
and are probably an interpolation.

a sin. Then shall the Assyrian fall with the sword, not of 8
man; and the sword, not of men, shall devour him: and
he shall flee from the sword, and his young men shall
become tributary. And his rock shall pass away by 9
reason of terror, and his princes shall be dismayed at the
ensign, saith the LORD, whose fire is in Zion, and his
furnace in Jerusalem.

xxxii. 1–8. *The Messianic regeneration of society.*

Behold, a king shall reign in righteousness, and princes **32**
shall rule in judgement. And a man shall be as an 2
hiding place from the wind, and a covert from the
tempest; as rivers of water in a dry place, as the
shadow of a great rock in a weary land. And the eyes of 3
them that see shall not be dim, and the ears of them that
hear shall hearken. The heart also of the rash shall 4

---

8. The continuation of *v.* 5. Yahwe Himself, and not the
Jews or Egyptians, will destroy the Assyrians.

9. And his rock...terror. The meaning is quite uncertain.
Perhaps ' he shall pass by his rock (stronghold or refuge) from
terror,' as a hunted animal may in the terror of the chase miss
its wonted hiding-place.

his princes...ensign: rather 'his officers will fly panic-stricken
from the standard.'

fire...furnace: an allusion, probably, to the Temple-altar.
Cf. ' altar-hearth,' xxix. 1.

VI. Ch. xxxii. 1–8.

The style of this passage is in some respects unlike that of
Isaiah, but there is no cogent reason for denying the authenticity
of *vv.* 1–5. There is no immediate connection with the preceding oracle.

1, 2. The governing classes will be animated by a new
spirit of righteousness and helpfulness.

2. a man: rather 'each one' (of the rulers).

tempest: ' rain-storm.'

3, 4. The mass of the people will no longer lack moral and
spiritual insight and susceptibility.

3. dim: marg. 'closed' (lit. 'smeared'), as in vi. 10, xxix. 10.

4. There will be no more hasty, ill-considered talk. Every
man will have sense and wisdom, and none will lack the power
of lucid speech.

understand knowledge, and the tongue of the stammerers
5 shall be ready to speak plainly.   The vile person shall be
no more called liberal, nor the churl said to be bountiful.
6 For the vile person will speak villany, and his heart will
work iniquity, to practise profaneness, and to utter error
against the LORD, to make empty the soul of the hungry,
7 and to cause the drink of the thirsty to fail.   The instruments also of the churl are evil: he deviseth wicked
devices to destroy the meek with lying words, even when
8 the needy speaketh right.   But the liberal deviseth
liberal things; and in liberal things shall he continue.

9-14.   *The impending desolation of Jerusalem.*

9   Rise up, ye women that are at ease, *and* hear my voice;

---

5.   Social distinctions will be based on character alone.

vile person...liberal...churl: marg. 'fool (such as Nabal
[=fool] in 1 Sam. xxv.)...noble (in rank)...crafty.' The meaning
of the last word is doubtful.

bountiful: another doubtful word; perhaps ' of good position '
(in society).

6-8.   The contrasted characters of the fool and the noble.
A didactic addition by a later hand.

6.   **For...iniquity**: render ' for the fool (here the blasphemous
atheist as in Ps. xiv. 1) speaks folly, and his heart meditates
(so LXX) mischief.'

7.   The knave is utterly unscrupulous in the means (' instruments,' a play upon the word for 'knave') by which he cheats
the poor out of their just rights.

VII.   Ch. xxxii. 9-20.

A minatory address to the fashionable women of Jerusalem
(*vv.* 9-14), followed by a delineation of the blessedness of the
Messianic age (*vv.* 15-20).

The denunciation is distinguished from the minatory discourses of this period (xxviii.-xxxi., c. 705-701) by the absence
of any definite allusion to the Assyrians, and by the threat of the
destruction and prolonged desolation of Jerusalem.   It recalls
Isaiah's earlier manner, e.g. iii. 16-iv. 1, v. 14 ff., with which,
rather than with xxix. 1-8, xxxi., it should be classed.   The
connection at *v.* 15 with the Messianic passage is in appearance
a close one, but the arrangement, as in the case of other
Messianic poems following denunciations, e.g. iv. 2 ff., ix. 2 ff.,

ye careless daughters, give ear unto my speech. For 10
days beyond a year shall ye be troubled, ye careless
women: for the vintage shall fail, the ingathering shall
not come. Tremble, ye women that are at ease; be 11
troubled, ye careless ones: strip you, and make you bare,
and gird *sackcloth* upon your loins. They shall smite 12
upon the breasts for the pleasant fields, for the fruitful vine.
Upon the land of my people shall come up thorns and 13
briers; yea, upon all the houses of joy in the joyous city:
for the palace shall be forsaken; the populous city shall be 14
deserted; the hill and the watch-tower shall be for dens
for ever, a joy of wild asses, a pasture of flocks;

15–20. *The bliss of the Messianic reign.*

until the spirit be poured upon us from on high, and the 15
wilderness become a fruitful field, and the fruitful field be
counted for a forest. Then judgement shall dwell in the 16
wilderness, and righteousness shall abide in the fruitful
field. And the work of righteousness shall be peace; 17

---

is probably editorial. There is no sufficient reason for question-
ing Isaiah's authorship of either part of the passage.

9. at ease...careless (marg. 'confident'): cf. Amos vi. 1.

10. For days...year: marg. 'after a year and days' (lit.
'days upon a year'), i.e. within an indefinite, but not prolonged,
space of time.

12, 13. Read 'Smite upon the breasts for...vine, for the
land of my people, which goes up in thorns and briers, yea, for
all the houses of gladness, the joyous city.'

14. the populous...deserted: 'the tumult of the city is a
solitude,' i.e. silence reigns in the place of the gay throngs.

the hill and the watch-tower. The word for 'hill' is Ophel,
the name of part of the Temple-hill, the aristocratic quarter of
the city. The 'watch-tower' (a doubtful word which does not
occur elsewhere) was also, doubtless, a familiar spot in the city.

a joy...flocks: cf. v. 17.

15. spirit: cf. xi. 2; Joel ii. 28.

and the wilderness...forest: see on xxix. 7.

17. work...effect: synonymous terms. The endowment of
the spirit enables men to carry out the will of God, and practise
righteousness. The result is quietness and confidence (xxx. 15),
and peace.

and the effect of righteousness quietness and confidence
18 for ever. And my people shall abide in a peaceable
habitation, and in sure dwellings, and in quiet resting
19 places. But it shall hail, in the downfall of the forest;
20 and the city shall be utterly laid low. Blessed are ye
that sow beside all waters, that send forth the feet of the
ox and the ass.

xxxiii. *The desolation and deliverance of Jerusalem.*

1-9. *The distress and complaint of the people.*

33   Woe to thee that spoilest, and thou wast not spoiled;
and dealest treacherously, and they dealt not treacherously
with thee! When thou hast ceased to spoil, thou shalt be
spoiled; and when thou hast made an end to deal treach-
2 erously, they shall deal treacherously with thee. O LORD,
be gracious unto us; we have waited for thee: be thou
their arm every morning, our salvation also in the time of

---

19.   This threat of judgment on Jerusalem is out of keeping
with the context, and has been interpolated or misplaced.
20.   The happy husbandman in the Messianic kingdom has
no lack of water for the irrigation of his fields, and his cattle
roam secure on the rich pastures.

VIII.   Ch. xxxiii.

This chapter, which depicts the distress of Jerusalem under
the cruelty of a treacherous foe, her deliverance by Yahwe, and
her future glory and prosperity, must refer, if Isaiah be its
author, to some treacherous act on the part of the Assyrians,
against whom retribution is threatened. It has usually been
referred to Sennacherib's attempt to secure possession of
Jerusalem, after having accepted Hezekiah's submission; but
its authenticity must be regarded as at least doubtful.
1.   spoilest...treacherously. The identity of the unnamed
foe is quite uncertain, whereas Isaiah's references to the
Assyrians are usually unmistakable. For the expressions cf.
xxi. 2, xxiv. 16.
2.   their: i.e. the people's, with special reference, perhaps, to
their fighting men.

trouble.   At the noise of the tumult the peoples are fled ; 3
at the lifting up of thyself the nations are scattered.   And 4
your spoil shall be gathered as the caterpiller gathereth :
as locusts leap shall they leap upon it.   The LORD is 5
exalted ; for he dwelleth on high : he hath filled Zion with
judgement and righteousness.   And there shall be stability 6
in thy times, abundance of salvation, wisdom and knowledge : the fear of the LORD is his treasure.

Behold, their valiant ones cry without : the ambassa- 7
dors of peace weep bitterly.   The high ways lie waste, 8
the wayfaring man ceaseth : he hath broken the covenant,
he hath despised the cities, he regardeth not man.   The 9
land mourneth and languisheth : Lebanon is ashamed
and withereth away : Sharon is like a desert ; and
Bashan and Carmel shake off *their leaves.*

10–13.   *Yahwe's response to His people's prayer.*

Now will I arise, saith the LORD ; now will I lift up myself ; 10
now will I be exalted.   Ye shall conceive chaff, ye shall 11
bring forth stubble : your breath is a fire that shall devour

---

3, 4.   Past experience of Divine aid leads to the assurance of
deliverance in the present crisis.

3.   **tumult**: the thunder, or other physical accompaniments
of Yahwe's intervention.

4.   **caterpiller...locusts**: rather 'locust...grasshopper.'

5.   Yahwe is exalted alike in power and in holiness.   His
moral qualities are reflected in the character of His faithful
people.

6.   The construction is obscure, and no translation is satisfactory.   Render, possibly, 'there shall be stability in thy times
(i.e. Jerusalem will enjoy peace and security); wisdom and
knowledge are a stone of salvation ; the fear of Yahwe is his
(Israel's) treasure.'

7.   **valiant ones.**   The word is utterly obscure, but the reference is presumably to the Jewish warriors who cry out in
indignant amazement at the enemy's treachery.

ambassadors of peace: the Jewish envoys who concluded
the treaty now broken by the enemy.

8.   **cities.**   The emendation 'witnesses' is preferable.

9.   The sympathy of nature.   Decay and desolation take the
place of luxuriant fertility.

12 you. And the peoples shall be as the burnings of lime: as thorns cut down, that are burned in the fire.

13 Hear, ye that are far off, what I have done; and, ye that are near, acknowledge my might.

14–16. The manifestation of Yahwe's power tests character and exposes disloyalty.

14 The sinners in Zion are afraid; trembling hath surprised the godless ones. Who among us shall dwell with the devouring fire? who among us shall dwell with everlasting

15 burnings? He that walketh righteously, and speaketh uprightly; he that despiseth the gain of oppressions, that shaketh his hands from holding of bribes, that stoppeth his ears from hearing of blood, and shutteth his eyes from

16 looking upon evil; he shall dwell on high: his place of defence shall be the munitions of rocks: his bread shall be given *him*; his waters shall be sure.

17–24. The future happiness of the redeemed Jerusalem.

17 Thine eyes shall see the king in his beauty: they shall

18 behold a far stretching land. Thine heart shall muse on the terror: where is he that counted, where is he that weighed *the tribute*? where is he that counted the towers?

---

12. **as...lime**: i.e. 'as if burnt to lime.'

14. **Who...burnings**: the anxious heart-searching question of the ungodly, who are now forced to recognize Yahwe's power and holiness. The Divine holiness is a consuming fire, and is eternal because an essential part of the Divine nature.

15, 16. The question in *v.* 14 is not strictly answered; but in contrast with the terror of the ungodly these verses depict the security and prosperity of the upright. Cf. Ps. xv. 1 ff., where, however, the question is general and the answer direct.

15. **hearing of blood**: becoming accessory to the shedding of blood.

17. The territory of the Messianic king will be of wide extent, no longer subject to the encroachments of hostile powers.

18. The dark days of oppression and terror will become but a memory. The foreign officials will disappear, and no enemy will scan the city's defences with a view to an assault.

Thou shalt not see the fierce people, a people of a deep 19
speech that thou canst not perceive ; of a strange tongue
that thou canst not understand.   Look upon Zion, the city 20
of our solemnities : thine eyes shall see Jerusalem a quiet
habitation, a tent that shall not be removed, the stakes
whereof shall never be plucked up, neither shall any of the
cords thereof be broken.   But there the LORD will be with 21
us in majesty, a place of broad rivers and streams ; wherein
shall go no galley with oars, neither shall gallant ship pass
thereby.   For the LORD is our judge, the LORD is our 22
lawgiver, the LORD is our king ; he will save us.   Thy 23
tacklings are loosed ; they could not strengthen the foot
of their mast, they could not spread the sail : then was
the prey of a great spoil divided ; the lame took the prey.
And the inhabitant shall not say, I am sick : the people 24
that dwell therein shall be forgiven their iniquity.

---

19.   The unintelligible speech of their foreign masters will no
longer sound in the ears of the people, constantly reminding
them of their servitude.   Cf. xxviii. 11.

20.   solemnities : rather ' festal assembly.'

21.   a place of : marg. ' in the place of.'   Instead of the
broad streams which flow past other capitals (e.g. the Nile or
Euphrates) Yahwe will be the glory and defence of His people,
a defence which, unlike the broad streams, is not open to attack.

23.   Thy tacklings...the sail.   The slackened ropes cannot hold
the mast in place, nor spread out the ensign (perhaps a flag, or,
as the use of flags on ships in ancient times is open to doubt, a
sail that might serve the purpose of an ensign ; cf. Ez. xxvii. 7).
If this be a description of the existing dismal state of Jerusalem,
which is compared to a helpless ship, the transition is intolerably
harsh.   More probably (in spite of *v.* 21), the verse describes
the fate of any foe who might attempt to attack the city, the
metaphor being suggested by *v.* 21.

was...divided...took : rather ' will be...divided...will take,'
when Yahwe intervenes to deliver His people.

24.   In the redeemed community sickness—a mark of the
Divine displeasure—will be unknown.

xxxiv., xxxv.   Yahwe's judgment, especially on Edom,
and the restoration of Israel.

xxxiv. 1-4.   The judgment on the world.

34   Come near, ye nations, to hear; and hearken, ye
peoples: let the earth hear, and the fulness thereof; the
2 world, and all things that come forth of it.   For the LORD
hath indignation against all the nations, and fury against
all their host: he hath utterly destroyed them, he hath
3 delivered them to the slaughter.   Their slain also shall be
cast out, and the stink of their carcases shall come up,
4 and the mountains shall be melted with their blood.   And
all the host of heaven shall be dissolved, and the heavens
shall be rolled together as a scroll: and all their host
shall fade away, as the leaf fadeth from off the vine, and
as a fading *leaf* from the fig tree.

IX.   Ch. xxxiv., xxxv.

These chapters, which are in the same rhythm, and doubtless
by the same hand, are post-exilic.   The exile and the dispersion
are clearly presupposed by ch. xxxv., and there is abundant
evidence of familiarity with exilic and post-exilic writings,
e.g. Is. xiii. f., xl.–lxvi., especially lxiii. 1-6.   The vehemence
of the Jewish hatred of Edom is accounted for by the manifestation of Edomitish hostility at the time of the fall of Jerusalem,
and finds frequent expression after that date, e.g. Ez. xxv. 12 ff.;
Obad. 10 ff.   A precise determination of the date of the passage
is impossible.

xxxiv. 1.   all...it: all the offspring of the earth, i.e. in this
case, its inhabitants.

2.   utterly destroyed: 'laid a ban upon,' marg. 'devoted'
(to destruction).   Cf. Deut. ii. 34, iii. 6.

4.   host of heaven: probably a gloss to 'their host' (i.e. the
stars) later in the verse, to distinguish this sense of the words
from that in *v.* 2.   The verbs 'melted,' *v.* 3, and 'dissolved,'
v. 4, are parallel, and their subjects should also be parallel,
while the heavens and their host form the subject of the
following clauses.   Read, therefore, 'and the hills shall be
dissolved.'

5–17. *The desolation of Edom.*

For my sword hath drunk its fill in heaven : behold, it 5
shall come down upon Edom, and upon the people of my
curse, to judgement. The sword of the LORD is filled 6
with blood, it is made fat with fatness, with the blood of
lambs and goats, with the fat of the kidneys of rams : for
the LORD hath a sacrifice in Bozrah, and a great slaughter in the land of Edom. And the wild-oxen shall come 7
down with them, and the bullocks with the bulls ; and
their land shall be drunken with blood, and their dust
made fat with fatness. For it is the day of the LORD's 8
vengeance, the year of recompence in the controversy of
Zion. And the streams thereof shall be turned into pitch, 9
and the dust thereof into brimstone, and the land thereof
shall become burning pitch. It shall not be quenched 10
night nor day ; the smoke thereof shall go up for ever :
from generation to generation it shall lie waste ; none shall
pass through it for ever and ever. But the pelican and the 11
porcupine shall possess it ; and the owl and the raven
shall dwell therein : and he shall stretch over it the line

---

5. drunk its fill : 'is drunk' (with fury), already prepared in
heaven for the slaughter to be wrought on earth.

curse : 'ban.' See on *v.* 2.

6. The Edomites, having been ceremonially devoted to destruction (*vv.* 2, 5), are compared to sacrificial victims.

made fat : made moist or greasy ; so also in *v.* 7.

Bozrah : a principal town of Edom, perhaps its capital
(cf. lxiii. 1), usually, but not with certainty, identified with
Buṣeira, south of the Dead Sea.

7. shall come down : rather 'are felled' by the slaughterer.

9, 10. The Divine vengeance takes the form of an unquench-
able fire covering the whole land.

the land thereof… : read (after LXX) 'its land shall
become pitch, burning night and day ; it is not quenched
for ever ; its smoke goes up from generation to generation ; it
lies waste to eternity, none passing through it.'

11 ff. Somewhat inconsistently the everlasting fire gives place
to a desolation, the haunt of beasts and demons.

11. porcupine : or 'bittern' ; see on xiv. 23.

12 of confusion, and the plummet of emptiness. They shall
call the nobles thereof to the kingdom, but none shall be
13 there ; and all her princes shall be nothing. And thorns
shall come up in her palaces, nettles and thistles in the
fortresses thereof : and it shall be an habitation of jackals,
14 a court for ostriches. And the wild beasts of the desert
shall meet with the wolves, and the satyr shall cry to his
fellow ; yea, the night-monster shall settle there, and
15 shall find her a place of rest. There shall the arrowsnake
make her nest, and lay, and hatch, and gather under her
shadow : yea, there shall the kites be gathered, every one
16 with her mate. Seek ye out of the book of the LORD,
and read : no one of these shall be missing, none shall
want her mate : for my mouth it hath commanded, and
17 his spirit it hath gathered them. And he hath cast the
lot for them, and his hand hath divided it unto them by
line : they shall possess it for ever, from generation to
generation shall they dwell therein.

---

12. They shall...there: rather 'her nobles...there is no
kingdom there which they may proclaim.' The text is defective, 'her nobles' being all that is left of an entire clause.
A possible restoration, based on LXX, is 'and satyrs shall
dwell in it; its nobles shall be nought; there is....'

13, 14. Cf. xiii. 21 f.

14. night-monster: Lilith, the night-hag, a female demon-
figure of the Babylonian mythology.

15. gather...shadow: i.e. gather her newly hatched brood
close to her. Another possible reading is 'gather her eggs.'

16. Seek...Lord: an appeal to later readers to study the
prophecy carefully in order to observe how literally it has been
fulfilled. The phrase implies the existence of a collection of
sacred writings of which this prophecy will form part, and thus
confirms the view that the passage is of late date.

my mouth: read 'the mouth of Yahwe.'

17. Yahwe Himself portions out Edom by lot to the beasts
and demons to be their eternal possession.

xxxv. *The everlasting joy of the redeemed Israel.*

The wilderness and the solitary place shall be glad ; **35**
and the desert shall rejoice, and blossom as the rose. It 2
shall blossom abundantly, and rejoice even with joy and
singing ; the glory of Lebanon shall be given unto it, the
excellency of Carmel and Sharon : they shall see the
glory of the LORD, the excellency of our God.

Strengthen ye the weak hands, and confirm the feeble 3
knees. Say to them that are of a fearful heart, Be strong, 4
fear not: behold, your God will come *with* vengeance,
with the recompence of God; he will come and save you.
Then the eyes of the blind shall be opened, and the ears 5
of the deaf shall be unstopped. Then shall the lame man 6
leap as an hart, and the tongue of the dumb shall sing :
for in the wilderness shall waters break out, and streams
in the desert. And the glowing sand shall become a pool, 7
and the thirsty ground springs of water : in the habitation
of jackals, where they lay, shall be grass with reeds and
rushes. And an high way shall be there, and a way, and 8

---

xxxv. The lurid picture of the desolating judgment is followed
by an idyllic representation of the happiness of Israel. The
abruptness of the transition adds point to the contrast.

1. solitary place: marg. 'parched land.'

rose: marg. 'autumn crocus'; cf. Cant. ii. 1.

4. fearful: marg. 'hasty,' as in xxxii. 4, where, however,
the sense is different. Here the meaning is 'quick to fall into
despair.'

behold...God: marg. 'Behold, your God! vengeance will
come, even the recompense of God.' For the expressions
cf. xl. 9 f.

5, 6. The language is not figurative merely, but implies the
healing of physical infirmities; cf. xxxiii. 24.

7. glowing sand: the cognate word in Arabic means
'mirage' (so marg. here and in xlix. 10, the only other place
in which the word occurs). But the rendering in the text
(so LXX) is supported by the parallel expression 'thirsty
ground' and by the unsuitability of 'mirage' in xlix. 10.

in...rushes: marg. 'court' instead of 'grass.' The text is
defective, and must be restored by conjecture, for which some

it shall be called The way of holiness ; the unclean shall
not pass over it ; but it shall be for those : the wayfaring
9 men, yea fools, shall not err *therein.* No lion shall be
there, nor shall any ravenous beast go up thereon, they
shall not be found there ; but the redeemed shall walk
10 *there* : and the ransomed of the LORD shall return, and
come with singing unto Zion ; and everlasting joy shall be
upon their heads : they shall obtain gladness and joy, and
sorrow and sighing shall flee away.

---

material is supplied by xxxiv. 13, to which this is clearly a com-
panion verse ; e.g. ' in the habitation of jackals shall lie (your
flocks?), and the court of ostriches shall become reeds and
rushes.'

8. The ' highway ' for the return of the exiles (xl. 3, xliii. 19,
xlix. 11 ; see also xi. 16) is here a permanent highway of pilgrimage. Cf. xix. 23.

but it...therein : read ' but it shall be for His people, when
it walks in the way (i.e. makes a pilgrimage); fools shall not live
in it.' The **fools** are the wicked, not the simple, and the
meaning is that the sacred highway will be free from their dis-
turbing presence, as from the pollution of the unclean (*v.* 8*a*),
and the peril of wild beasts (*v.* 9).

Ch. xxxvi.–xxxix. THE HISTORICAL APPENDIX.

These chapters narrate three incidents in the reign of Hezekiah,
in which Isaiah played a prominent part :—(*a*) the efforts of
Sennacherib to wring from Hezekiah the surrender of Jerusalem
(xxxvi., xxxvii.) ; (*b*) the king's sickness and recovery (xxxviii.) ;
(*c*) the embassy of Merodach-Baladan (xxxix.). The same
incidents are related, with slight modifications, in 2 Kings xviii.
13–xx. 19, the chief differences between the two accounts being
that that in Isaiah (1) omits to mention Hezekiah's submission
(2 Kings xviii. 13–16), (2) inserts Hezekiah's psalm of thanksgiving on his recovery (xxxviii. 9–20), and (3) shows a tendency
to abbreviation. It is probable that the stories formed part of a
biography (or biographies) of Isaiah, from which they were
incorporated in the book of Kings, from which again they were
appended, for the sake of convenient reference, to an edition of
Isaiah's prophecies. At what date the appendix was added
cannot be determined with certainty. It is not probable that
any portion of these chapters was written by Isaiah himself.

xxxvi., xxxvii. *Sennacherib's unsuccessful demand for the surrender of Jerusalem.*

Now it came to pass in the fourteenth year of king **36** Hezekiah, that Sennacherib king of Assyria came up against all the fenced cities of Judah, and took them. And the king of Assyria sent Rabshakeh from Lachish to **2**

---

xxxvi., xxxvii. These chapters contain, after the introductory verse xxxvi. 1 = 2 Kings xviii. 13, two parallel narratives of Sennacherib's attempt to obtain the surrender of Jerusalem, (α) xxxvi. 2–xxxvii. 9*a*, 37, 38 = 2 Kings xviii. 17–xix. 9*a*, 36, 37; (β) xxxvii. 9*b*–36 = 2 Kings xix. 9*b*–35. In the first narrative the demand that Jerusalem be surrendered is supported by a display of force (xxxvi. 2); it is rejected on the advice of Isaiah, who predicts that Sennacherib will hear a rumour and will return to his own land, where he will fall by the sword (xxxvii. 6, 7): this is fulfilled (xxxvii. 9*a* (to ' heard it'), 37, 38). In the second narrative the demand is made by letter (xxxvii. 14); Isaiah predicts that Sennacherib will not assault Jerusalem, but will return by the same way by which he came; and the cause of Sennacherib's retreat is the death (presumably by pestilence) of 185,000 of his army (xxxvii. 33–36). It is more probable that these are parallel narratives of the same event than that they describe two consecutive attempts—the second weaker than the first—to induce Hezekiah to surrender the city. The Assyrian account of the campaign agrees closely with 2 Kings xviii. 13–16, but gives no explanation of the failure to reduce Jerusalem. These narratives give the Hebrew traditions as to the cause of Sennacherib's retreat.

xxxvi. 1. The statement that Sennacherib's invasion (701 B.C.) took place in the fourteenth year of Hezekiah conflicts with that of 2 Kings xviii. 10 that Samaria fell (721 B.C.) in Hezekiah's sixth year. The question of the date of Hezekiah's accession is an intricate one. Note, however, that these chapters appear to imply (xxxviii. 1) that Sennacherib's invasion and Hezekiah's sickness were roughly contemporaneous. As Hezekiah's life is said to have been prolonged for 15 years after his sickness, and as his reign lasted 29 years (2 Kings xviii. 2), the statement that these incidents occurred in his fourteenth year is the result of a simple calculation, and has little independent value.

2. Rabshakeh: an Assyrian official title, probably 'chief of the officers.'

Jerusalem unto king Hezekiah with a great army. And
he stood by the conduit of the upper pool in the high way
3 of the fuller's field. Then came forth unto him Eliakim
the son of Hilkiah, which was over the household, and
Shebna the scribe, and Joah the son of Asaph the
4 recorder. And Rabshakeh said unto them, Say ye now
to Hezekiah, Thus saith the great king, the king of
Assyria, What confidence is this wherein thou trustest?
5 I say, *thy* counsel and strength for the war are but vain
words: now on whom dost thou trust, that thou hast
6 rebelled against me? Behold, thou trustest upon the
staff of this bruised reed, even upon Egypt; whereon if a
man lean, it will go into his hand, and pierce it: so is
7 Pharaoh king of Egypt to all that trust on him. But if
thou say unto me, We trust in the LORD our God: is not
that he, whose high places and whose altars Hezekiah
hath taken away, and hath said to Judah and to Jerusalem,
8 Ye shall worship before this altar? Now therefore, I pray
thee, give pledges to my master the king of Assyria, and
I will give thee two thousand horses, if thou be able on
9 thy part to set riders upon them. How then canst thou
turn away the face of one captain of the least of my
master's servants, and put thy trust on Egypt for chariots
10 and for horsemen? And am I now come up without the
LORD against this land to destroy it? The LORD said

Lachish: south-west of Jerusalem towards Gaza; the modern
Tell el-Hasi.

conduit...field: see on vii. 3.

3. Eliakim...Shebna: see on xxii. 15–25.

4 ff. The speeches put into the mouth of the Rabshakeh are
drawn partly from Isaiah's oracles. He echoes Isaiah's language
about the Egyptian alliance (*v.* 6), and represents Sennacherib
as Yahwe's instrument (*v.* 10). Cf. also *vv.* 18–20 with x. 8–11.

7. Cf. 2 Kings xviii. 4.

8. give pledges to: marg. 'make a wager with.' The Rabshakeh derisively offers to furnish 2000 horses if Hezekiah can
find 2000 cavalrymen to ride them. See on xxxi. 1.

unto me, Go up against this land, and destroy it. Then 11
said Eliakim and Shebna and Joah unto Rabshakeh,
Speak, I pray thee, unto thy servants in the Syrian
language ; for we understand it : and speak not to us in
the Jews' language, in the ears of the people that are on
the wall. But Rabshakeh said, Hath my master sent me to 12
thy master, and to thee, to speak these words? *hath he* not
sent me to the men that sit upon the wall, to eat their own
dung, and to drink their own water with you? Then 13
Rabshakeh stood, and cried with a loud voice in the Jews'
language, and said, Hear ye the words of the great king,
the king of Assyria.   Thus saith the king, Let not 14
Hezekiah deceive you ; for he shall not be able to deliver
you : neither let Hezekiah make you trust in the LORD, 15
saying, The LORD will surely deliver us ; this city shall
not be given into the hand of the king of Assyria.
Hearken not to Hezekiah : for thus saith the king of 16
Assyria, Make your peace with me, and come out to me ;
and eat ye every one of his vine, and every one of his fig
tree, and drink ye every one the waters of his own
cistern : until I come and take you away to a land like 17
your own land, a land of corn and wine, a land of bread
and vineyards.   Beware lest Hezekiah persuade you, 18
saying, The LORD will deliver us.   Hath any of the gods
of the nations delivered his land out of the hand of the
king of Assyria? Where are the gods of Hamath and 19
Arpad? where are the gods of Sepharvaim? and have they
delivered Samaria out of my hand?   Who are they 20
among all the gods of these countries, that have delivered
their country out of my hand, that the LORD should

---

12. The dire consequences to the people of siding with their
own rulers ('with you') against the Assyrians.   Note the contrast in *v.* 16 f.

19. Hamath and Arpad : see on x. 9.

Sepharvaim : possibly identical with Sibraim (Ez. xlvii. 16)
between Hamath and Damascus.

21 deliver Jerusalem out of my hand? But they held their
peace, and answered him not a word : for the king's
22 commandment was, saying, Answer him not. Then came
Eliakim the son of Hilkiah, that was over the household,
and Shebna the scribe, and Joah the son of Asaph the
recorder, to Hezekiah with their clothes rent, and told him
the words of Rabshakeh.

37   And it came to pass, when king Hezekiah heard it, that
he rent his clothes, and covered himself with sackcloth,
2 and went into the house of the LORD. And he sent
Eliakim, who was over the household, and Shebna the
scribe, and the elders of the priests, covered with sack-
3 cloth, unto Isaiah the prophet the son of Amoz. And
they said unto him, Thus saith Hezekiah, This day is a
day of trouble, and of rebuke, and of contumely : for the
children are come to the birth, and there is not strength
4 to bring forth. It may be the LORD thy God will hear
the words of Rabshakeh, whom the king of Assyria his
master hath sent to reproach the living God, and will
rebuke the words which the LORD thy God hath heard :
wherefore lift up thy prayer for the remnant that is left.
5
6 So the servants of king Hezekiah came to Isaiah. And
Isaiah said unto them, Thus shall ye say to your master,
Thus saith the LORD, Be not afraid of the words that
thou hast heard, wherewith the servants of the king of
7 Assyria have blasphemed me. Behold, I will put a spirit
in him, and he shall hear a rumour, and shall return unto
his own land ; and I will cause him to fall by the sword
in his own land.
8   So Rabshakeh returned, and found the king of Assyria

---

xxxvii. 3. trouble...contumely : rather ' distress and chastisement and rejection (by God). '

the children...forth: a proverbial expression for inability to
meet a crisis.

7. a spirit : i.e. of cowardice.

warring against Libnah : for he had heard that he was
departed from Lachish.   And he heard say concerning 9
Tirhakah king of Ethiopia, He is come out to fight
against thee.   And when he heard it, he sent messengers
to Hezekiah, saying, Thus shall ye speak to Hezekiah 10
king of Judah, saying, Let not thy God in whom thou
trustest deceive thee, saying, Jerusalem shall not be given
into the hand of the king of Assyria.   Behold, thou hast 11
heard what the kings of Assyria have done to all lands,
by destroying them utterly : and shalt thou be delivered ?
Have the gods of the nations delivered them, which my 12
fathers have destroyed, Gozan, and Haran, and Rezeph,
and the children of Eden which were in Telassar ? Where 13
is the king of Hamath, and the king of Arpad, and the
king of the city of Sepharvaim, of Hena, and Ivvah ?
And Hezekiah received the letter from the hand of the 14
messengers, and read it : and Hezekiah went up unto the
house of the LORD, and spread it before the LORD.   And 15
Hezekiah prayed unto the LORD, saying, O LORD of hosts, 16
the God of Israel, that sittest upon the cherubim, thou art
the God, even thou alone, of all the kingdoms of the
earth ; thou hast made heaven and earth.   Incline thine 17
ear, O LORD, and hear ; open thine eyes, O LORD, and
see : and hear all the words of Sennacherib, which hath
sent to reproach the living God.   Of a truth, LORD, the 18

---

8.   **Libnah** : an unidentified town near Lachish.
9.   **when he heard it.**   The news of the approach of Tirhakah
is the 'rumour' (*v.* 7).   The sentence is completed in *v.* 37.

he sent messengers : the second of the parallel narratives,
the introductory words of which have been lost in the process of
amalgamation.
12.   **Gozan** and **Haran** (Carrhae) were in northern Mesopo-
tamia.   **Rezeph** (Rusafa) lay slightly south of the Euphrates,
near Sura, on the way from Haran to Palmyra.

children...Telassar : a small kingdom, Bit-Adini (**Eden**), on
the upper Euphrates.
13.   For **Hamath, Arpad,** and **Sepharvaim** see xxxvi. 19.
Hena and **Ivvah** were unidentified Syrian towns.

kings of Assyria have laid waste all the countries, and
19 their land, and have cast their gods into the fire: for
they were no gods, but the work of men's hands, wood
20 and stone; therefore they have destroyed them. Now
therefore, O LORD our God, save us from his hand, that
all the kingdoms of the earth may know that thou art the
LORD, even thou only.

21   Then Isaiah the son of Amoz sent unto Hezekiah,
saying, Thus saith the LORD, the God of Israel, Whereas
thou hast prayed to me against Sennacherib king of
22 Assyria, this is the word which the LORD hath spoken
concerning him: The virgin daughter of Zion hath
despised thee and laughed thee to scorn; the daughter of
23 Jerusalem hath shaken her head at thee. Whom hast thou
reproached and blasphemed? and against whom hast
thou exalted thy voice and lifted up thine eyes on high?
24 *even* against the Holy One of Israel. By thy servants
hast thou reproached the Lord, and hast said, With the
multitude of my chariots am I come up to the height
of the mountains, to the innermost parts of Lebanon;
and I will cut down the tall cedars thereof, and the
choice fir trees thereof: and I will enter into his
25 farthest height, the forest of his fruitful field. I have
digged and drunk water, and with the sole of my feet
26 will I dry up all the rivers of Egypt. Hast thou not
heard how I have done it long ago, and formed it of

---

22. Isaiah's message, *vv.* 21, 33-35, is interrupted by the
insertion of a taunt-song on Sennacherib in the Ḳinah rhythm
(see on i. 21), *vv.* 22-29, to which is appended a prediction to
Hezekiah, *vv.* 30-32.

25. water: read 'foreign water' as in 2 Kings xix. 24.
Cf. Prov. ix. 17.

and with...Egypt: an empty boast in the mouth of Sennacherib, as the first invasion of Egypt took place under his
successor.

26-29. The Assyrian has been but an instrument in the hand
of Yahwe, before whom he himself is helpless.

ancient times? now have I brought it to pass, that thou shouldest be to lay waste fenced cities into ruinous heaps. Therefore their inhabitants were of small power, they 27 were dismayed and confounded; they were as the grass of the field, and as the green herb, as the grass on the housetops, and as a field *of corn* before it be grown up. But I know thy sitting down, and thy going out, and thy 28 coming in, and thy raging against me. Because of thy 29 raging against me, and for that thine arrogancy is come up into mine ears, therefore will I put my hook in thy nose, and my bridle in thy lips, and I will turn thee back by the way by which thou camest. And this shall be the 30 sign unto thee: ye shall eat this year that which groweth of itself, and in the second year that which springeth of the same; and in the third year sow ye, and reap, and plant vineyards, and eat the fruit thereof. And the remnant 31 that is escaped of the house of Judah shall again take root downward, and bear fruit upward. For out of Jerusalem 32 shall go forth a remnant, and out of mount Zion they that shall escape: the zeal of the LORD of hosts shall perform this. Therefore thus saith the LORD concerning the king 33 of Assyria, He shall not come unto this city, nor shoot an arrow there, neither shall he come before it with shield, nor cast a mount against it. By the way that he came, 34 by the same shall he return, and he shall not come unto this city, saith the LORD. For I will defend this city to 35 save it, for mine own sake, and for my servant David's sake.

27*b*, 28. before it...coming in: read 'before the east wind. Before me (=known to me) is thy uprising and thy sitting down; thy going out and thy coming in I know.'

30. The prediction is addressed to Hezekiah. The Assyrians have ravaged the land so thoroughly that two years will pass before it yields a full crop.

32. the zeal...this: a reminiscence of ix. 7.

33-35. The continuation of *v.* 21.

36   And the angel of the LORD went forth, and smote in
      the camp of the Assyrians a hundred and fourscore and
      five thousand : and when men arose early in the morning,
37 behold, they were all dead corpses.   So Sennacherib king
      of Assyria departed, and went and returned, and dwelt at
38 Nineveh.   And it came to pass, as he was worshipping in
      the house of Nisroch his god, that Adrammelech and
      Sharezer his sons smote him with the sword : and they
      escaped into the land of Ararat.   And Esar-haddon his
      son reigned in his stead.

xxxviii.   *Hezekiah's sickness and recovery.*

38   In those days was Hezekiah sick unto death.   And
      Isaiah the prophet the son of Amoz came to him, and
      said unto him, Thus saith the LORD, Set thine house in
 2 order ; for thou shalt die, and not live.   Then Hezekiah
      turned his face to the wall, and prayed unto the LORD,
 3 and said, Remember now, O LORD, I beseech thee, how I
      have walked before thee in truth and with a perfect heart,
      and have done that which is good in thy sight.   And
 4 Hezekiah wept sore.   Then came the word of the LORD

---

36.   The Hebrew tradition that the cause of Sennacherib's
return to Assyria was an appalling outbreak of plague among
his troops receives some confirmation from the mention in
Herodotus II. 141 of a disaster to the Assyrian army (in
Pelusium, in Egypt) in the shape of a plague of field-mice,
which may be the symbol of pestilence.   What the precise
disaster was, where it occurred, and to what extent it was
responsible for Sennacherib's return, are matters of conjecture.
The Assyrian record is, naturally enough, silent on the point.

37 f.   The conclusion of the first narrative (see *v.* 9).

38.   Sennacherib was assassinated in 681 B.C.   There is no
other mention of an Assyrian god Nisroch, and the name is
possibly a corruption of Assur, or of Nusku, a lesser deity.

xxxviii. 1.   In those days.   The present order of the incidents
is not chronological (see on xxxvi. 1), and the indication of date
is quite vague.   The narrative may have had a different context
in the biography of Isaiah from which these chapters are drawn.

2.   turned...wall.   He turns away from his immediate surroundings that he may feel himself to be alone with God.

to Isaiah, saying, Go, and say to Hezekiah, Thus saith 5
the LORD, the God of David thy father, I have heard
thy prayer, I have seen thy tears : behold, I will add unto
thy days fifteen years. And I will deliver thee and this 6
city out of the hand of the king of Assyria : and I will
defend this city. And this shall be the sign unto thee 7
from the LORD, that the LORD will do this thing that he
hath spoken : behold, I will cause the shadow on the steps, 8
which is gone down on the dial of Ahaz with the sun, to
return backward ten steps. So the sun returned ten steps
on the dial whereon it was gone down.

The writing of Hezekiah king of Judah, when he had 9
been sick, and was recovered of his sickness.

I said, In the noontide of my days I shall go into the 10
gates of the grave :
I am deprived of the residue of my years.
I said, I shall not see the LORD, *even* the LORD in the 11
land of the living :
I shall behold man no more with the inhabitants of the
world.

---

5. fifteen years : see on xxxvi. 1.
6. This promise was probably inserted (from xxxvii. 35 ;
cf. 2 Kings xx. 6) on the assumption that Hezekiah's sickness
was contemporaneous with Sennacherib's invasion.
8. steps...sun : read 'steps which the sun has gone down
on the dial of Ahaz.'
dial. The construction of the sun-dial and the method of
marking the passage of time are unknown.
9-20. Hezekiah's psalm of thanksgiving. The psalm does
not appear in the parallel narrative in 2 Kings xx., and was
doubtless inserted here as being suitable to Hezekiah's circumstances.
9. writing : possibly, with a change of one letter in Hebrew,
'Michtam' (Pss. xvi., lvi.-lx.), a psalm-title of uncertain
meaning.
10. noontide : lit. 'rest,' usually interpreted, as in R.V., to
mean 'noontide,' either because the heat of the day was the time
for rest, or because at that time the sun appears to rest in the
zenith.

12   Mine age is removed, and is carried away from me as a
        shepherd's tent :

      I have rolled up like a weaver my life ; he will cut me
        off from the loom :

      From day even to night wilt thou make an end of me.

13   I quieted *myself* until morning ; as a lion, so he break-
        eth all my bones :

      From day even to night wilt thou make an end of me.

14   Like a swallow *or* a crane, so did I chatter ;

      I did mourn as a dove: mine eyes fail *with looking*
        upward ;

      O LORD, I am oppressed, be thou my surety.

15   What shall I say ? he hath both spoken unto me, and
        himself hath done it :

      I shall go softly all my years because of the bitterness
        of my soul.

---

12. age : marg. ' habitation.'

I have...loom : the life that is being cut short is like a finished
web which is rolled up by the weaver, and severed from the
thrum (marg.), or thread by which the web is attached to the
loom.

From day...night : perhaps = ' within a short time, not more
than a day or night,' but the clause is obscure. Read, possibly,
' day and night am I abandoned (to pain).'

13. I quieted myself : read ' I cried.'

14. or a crane : omit, with LXX. The verb ' chirp ' does
not suit the crane, which was probably introduced into the text
from Jer. viii. 7.

upward : to God, in prayer for help.

surety : against death, figured as an oppressive creditor about
to seize the person of the debtor.

15, 16. Two obscure verses with corrupt text. The sense of
R.V. is ' God has spoken (by the prophet) and has healed me.
Henceforth I shall live securely because of the promise granted
during this bitter experience. By such acts of Divine grace men
live, and my spirit is quickened.' But this rendering strains the
words. Conjectural emendation yields the good sense ' What
shall I speak and say to Him?—for it is He that has done it
(brought this sickness upon me) ; I toss restlessly all my sleeping-
time because of the bitterness of my soul. Lord, therefore my

O Lord, by these things men live,   16
And wholly therein is the life of my spirit:
Wherefore recover thou me, and make me to live.
Behold, *it was* for *my* peace *that* I had great bitter- 17
 ness:
But thou hast in love to my soul delivered it from the
 pit of corruption;
For thou hast cast all my sins behind thy back.
For the grave cannot praise thee, death cannot celebrate 18
 thee:
They that go down into the pit cannot hope for thy
 truth.
The living, the living, he shall praise thee, as I do this 19
 day:
The father to the children shall make known thy truth.
The LORD is *ready* to save me: 20
Therefore we will sing my songs to the stringed instru-
 ments
All the days of our life in the house of the LORD.

Now Isaiah had said, Let them take a cake of figs, and 21
lay it for a plaister upon the boil, and he shall recover.
Hezekiah also had said, What is the sign that I shall go 22
up to the house of the LORD?

---

heart waits upon Thee.   Revive my spirit, and recover me, and
give me health.'
   17.   **thou...corruption**: read 'Thou hast kept back my soul
from the pit of destruction.'
   18.   Cf. Ps. vi. 5, xxx. 9, lxxxviii. 10–12, cxv. 17.
   20.   A liturgical addition, adapting the psalm for congre-
gational use. Note the change to 1st pers. plur.
   21, 22.   These verses are misplaced and should precede *v.* 7.
They are probably a marginal gloss from 2 Kings xx. 7 f. For
'now Isaiah had said...Hezekiah also had said' read 'and
Isaiah said...and Hezekiah said.'

xxxix. *The embassy of Merodach-Baladan.*

39 At that time Merodach-baladan the son of Baladan,
king of Babylon, sent letters and a present to Hezekiah :
for he heard that he had been sick, and was recovered.
2 And Hezekiah was glad of them, and shewed them the
house of his precious things, the silver, and the gold,
and the spices, and the precious oil, and all the
house of his armour, and all that was found in his
treasures : there was nothing in his house, nor in all his
3 dominion, that Hezekiah shewed them not. Then came
Isaiah the prophet unto king Hezekiah, and said unto him,
What said these men? and from whence came they unto
thee? And Hezekiah said, They are come from a far
4 country unto me, even from Babylon. Then said he,
What have they seen in thine house? And Hezekiah
answered, All that is in mine house have they seen : there
is nothing among my treasures that I have not shewed
5 them. Then said Isaiah to Hezekiah, Hear the word of
6 the LORD of hosts. Behold, the days come, that all that

---

xxxix. Merodach-Baladan made himself master of Babylonia
in 721 B.C. and ruled until c. 709, when he was driven out by
Sargon. In 704 he again obtained possession of Babylonia,
but was finally overthrown by Sennacherib after a reign of not
more than nine months. Whether, therefore, this embassy was
sent during his first or second tenure of power, this chapter
must chronologically precede xxxvi., xxxvii. The first verse
of the chapter connects the embassy with Hezekiah's recovery,
but Merodach-Baladan's object was clearly political, and the
chronological data of these chapters are insecure (see on
xxxvi. 1), so that little stress can be laid on xxxix. 1 in
determining the date of the embassy, which was probably sent
during Merodach-Baladan's earlier reign of 12 years.
2. The display of wealth and armour had the object of
encouraging Merodach-Baladan in the hope of assistance from
Judah against Assyria.
5–7. The rebuke is strangely unlike the genuine utterances
of Isaiah. Instead of a warning against the foolish policy of
resistance to Assyria, there is a prophecy of remote disaster,

is in thine house, and that which thy fathers have laid up
in store until this day, shall be carried to Babylon:
nothing shall be left, saith the LORD.   And of thy sons 7
that shall issue from thee, which thou shalt beget, shall
they take away; and they shall be eunuchs in the palace
of the king of Babylon.   Then said Hezekiah unto Isaiah, 8
Good is the word of the LORD which thou hast spoken.
He said moreover, For there shall be peace and truth in
my days.

---

which can hardly be reconciled with Isaiah's anticipations of
Divine intervention, and the establishment of the Messianic
kingdom after the overthrow of Assyria.   The tradition has
been edited in the light of subsequent events.

    8.   Hezekiah receives with pious resignation the prediction of
a calamity which will not affect him personally.   The postpone-
ment of disaster was regarded as a mitigation of its severity;
cf. 1 Kings xxi. 28 f.

INDEX

For EU product safety concerns, contact us at Calle de José Abascal, 56–1°,
28003 Madrid, Spain or eugpsr@cambridge.org.

www.ingramcontent.com/pod-product-compliance
Ingram Content Group UK Ltd.
Pitfield, Milton Keynes, MK11 3LW, UK
UKHW020310140625
459647UK00018B/1820